Pyramid Power and its healing abilities.

Pyramid Power and its use in achieving deep states of altered consciousness and stress free-high energy meditations.

Pyramid Power and its relationship to Black Holes in space.

Pyramid Power as an electronic healing field that can assist in rejuvenation of the human body.

PYRAMID POWER A NEW REALITY

... is a revised and updated version of the book *Pyramids a Second Reality*. This updated version also contains photographs and other material taken from the video program of the same name ("Pyramid Power a New Reality", still photos by Carole Joyce).

PYRAMID POWER

A NEW REALITY

**Bill Schul, Ph.D.,
and Ed Pettit**

STILLPOINT • WALPOLE, N.H.

ISBN 0-913-299-41-3

This book is published by
Stillpoint
Box 477 Meeting House Rd
Walpole, N.H. 03608

Printed & bound in Canada

CONTENTS

PYRAMIDS

AND THE
SECOND REALITY

It has been fifteen years since we were told that one of the major secrets of the Great Pyramid resides in its shape.

The great stone structure standing on the Egyptian plains at Giza for longer than history can remember has witnessed man's struggles upon this earth. It was there to haunt man's search for the meaning of life centuries before Moses and Buddha and Christ were to offer us answers. And it stands now — awesome and unchanged by time — watching us unlease our space-age dreams. It is not too difficult to imagine a world centuries from now altered beyond our visions and still in the midst of it all the Great Pyramid standing silent sentry.

Is it beyond our ability to comprehend its meaning, its reason for being? What philosophical or cosmological mysteries was it intended to reveal? But of all the hidden knowledge perhaps therein contained, one clue emerged and it offered information of considerable value . . . large or small containers made according to the proportions of the Great Pyramid create or capture within them energy force fields different than those in any other enclosed space.

Their imagination fired by this information, thousands of accredited researchers and basement experimenters, working with everything from three inch cardboard models to large pyramid homes, discovered for themselves that the environment within a pyramid was indeed special.

It has been found that this unusual energy affects living systems, plant to human, and will alter the molecular structure of liquids and solids. What is this energy? It includes, of course, components of the electromagnetic spectrum and perhaps in unique combinations, but the research would indicate that there are other forces involved of which little is known. Some have suggested that the pyramid acts as an antenna drawing in and focusing various force fields while others view the pyramid as a generator and still others see the pyramid as an amplifier of existing energies.

Obviously, in spite of the extensive research, a great deal remains to be learned. Perhaps we have only scratched the surface. We invite you to join us in this adventure. The price is right for your experiments can be launche with a few pieces of cardboard or wood.

In the pages that follow we will share some of our explorations and ideas about the nature of pyramids and how we think they perform. At the back of the book is a special section that evolved from a unique project. As a result of the great interest generated by the investigation of pyramid energy and the communications from people stating they wanted to become involved in this adventure, we decided to share the excitement of how to construct and use pyramids in the most graphic way possible . . . through video. This film guides the experimenter step-by-step through all stages of construction and setting up of experiments.

If you choose to join us in these fascinating and worthwhile investigations, you will find that we are in the company of a growing number of scientists. Technology has now reached that point in time when it can examine low-energy force fields. With this development we are learning that we live in a sea of energy where everything affects everything and the separation between substances is not empty space as imagined even a few years ago. The pyramid and its rich interior environment fits well into this unfolding picture of worlds within worlds.

HOW was a mentally retarded child helped by using a pyramid?

Why do some materials lose weight inside of pyramids?

Are there particles which move faster than the speed of light? Negative space-time? Antimatter? Is the pyramid a bridge between our world and other realities?

What have experiments with laser beams revealed about the forces within pyramids?

What does a pyramid have in common with a black hole in space?

What assurance do we have that pyramid effects are beneficial to man?

Why are pyramids with indented sides more effective than pyramids with flat sides?

Why was the King's Chamber not in the center of the Great Pyramid?

Why was the roof over the King's Chamber gabled? Does a laser beam reveal the reason?

Does exposure to pyramid space actually promote rejuvenation of the human body?

Questions at random? Questions raised on the opening pages of a book to lead the reader to believe that the answers to all of the questions he ever wanted to ask about pyramids are contained herein? The answer to both questions is "no." The authors do not suggest for a moment that the answers to the enigma of pyramid energy are neatly wrapped up and ready for presentation to the reader on the pages that follow. However, the above questions were carefully chosen, for they represent subjects on which new experiments and research offer findings, some exciting breakthroughs, and more than a little insight.

The research with pyramid models can no longer be called a fad. Too many people throughout the world are involved in pyramid research and experimentation to consider the matter as other than serious. Pyramid studies are not fun and games. Those were over the day we—and thousands of others—discovered that pyramid effects were repeatable phenomena. Too many people are using pyramids in a variety of practical ways, with some now living in pyramid homes, and too many laboratories are involved in investigating the forces at work in pyramids for any informed person to contend that pyramid space is the same as any other space.

Witness the United States patent issued to NASA for a collector of cosmic energies—collectors made of a series of pyramid shapes...

Witness the findings which indicate that radioactive isotopes lose their radioactivity in less time inside of a pyramid...

Witness the farm bulletin issued by the United States Department of Agriculture reporting on a study which revealed that thirty-inch pyramids placed in pastures reduced flies and other flying pests of livestock by seventy percent...

Witness the United States patent issued for pyramid-shaped loudspeakers...

We believe that pyramid research has vast implications. More than likely only the surface has been scratched, but we feel that the readers will be somewhat awed by how far the field has developed since the fledgling days of surprise when a treated razor blade actually did produce more shaves.

The results of pyramid research are sufficiently

exciting that there is little call for sensationalism or
misleading information. There is as great a need for
integrity and honest reporting here as in any other realm
of scientific exploration. Facts are herein presented and
where we have speculated on the nature, meaning, or
implications of the findings, it is so indicated. Our
conclusions are not necessarily the correct ones, but they
are the best that we have to offer at this moment in time
and the space that we occupy. Perhaps the reader will
arrive at different conclusions. If so, we can all benefit
from the exchange. It is not difficult to imagine that this,
too, was one of the purposes behind the construction of
the Great Pyramid.

ONE

Fever of the Unknown

LITTLE did we dream when we placed our first razor blade inside our first small pyramid model that we would be embarking on an adventure which would in five years sweep more than five million people in this country alone into the mysterious realm of pyramids. Caught in the fever of exploring an unknown—one that partook of both the sane but limited findings of science and the sometimes questionable but uninhibited flights of the occult—individuals from every walk of life were to discover that effects produced by pyramids were not an alchemist's impossible dream.

As what appeared on first encounter to be the irrational turned into logic and demonstrable reality, the experimenters sharpened their razor blades, processed their food and water, grew plants, germinated seeds, and sat, slept, meditated, and even lived inside of pyramids. They were not to join the ranks of the disenchanted. Their pyramids worked. When occasionally they did not, the reason was usually found to be faulty construction, misalignment, the presence of strong electrical fields, or the inhibiting factor of being housed in rooms with too much metal.

We started our experiments to satisfy our own curiosities. Comfortable with the experience that something unusual was happening within pyramid space, we shared these experiences in *The Secret Power of Pyramids*. We were pleasantly surprised with reader response to the book and sales soon mounted into the hundreds of thousands in this and several other countries. But our writing of the second book, *The Psychic Power of Pyramids,* was not generated by the success of the first book. Pyramid research by us and others continued unabated and a second book was required in order to report on new findings. And now this book is being written because continued experiments have produced additional and important data. We have no way of knowing at this point in time whether we will do additional writing about pyramids. That remains to be seen. We are reasonably certain, however, that our experiments with models of the Great Pyramid of Giza will continue for some time to come. More than likely, we and other investigators have merely scratched the surface of a field of study which shows every promise of making a serious contribution to knowledge in several

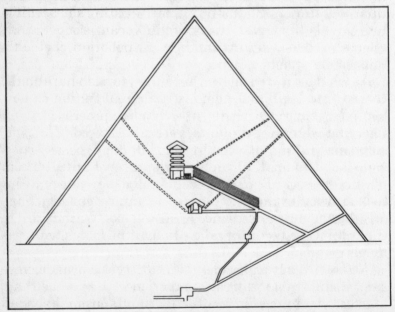

Drawing showing interior of Great Pyramid.

areas. While it appears at first flush to be ambitious to suggest that pyramid research has application to studies in history, archaeology, mythology, religion, physics, engineering, architecture, psychology, mathematics, and medicine, it becomes less grandiose when we remember that knowledge seldom falls into the private domain of a single discipline.

Learning more about the Great Pyramid—how it was constructed, by whom, and for what purpose or purposes—provides information of value to historians, anthropologists, theologians, architects, engineers, mathematicians, to name only some. The effects produced by pyramid models on solids, liquids, gases, and living organisms of the plant and animal kingdoms are of interest to just about everybody. And the results recorded on the physical, emotional, and mental states of people have a particular interest to philosophers, physicians, and psychologists. The energy crisis and the current demand for new energy sources have focused public attention on possible alternatives to existing sources. It is premature to suggest that pyramids can produce sufficient usable energy to make a contribution. Yet, this possibility should not be overlooked, and if one of the answers does not reside within the pyramid shape itself, it may be that it will make a real contribution to new understanding concerning the nature of energy. In any case, the closer we study the accomplishments of ancient builders the more we suspect that they possessed a knowledge of energy fields which we have yet to obtain. This suspicion not only adds the thrill of mystery to our search but also the very practical pursuit of a knowledge which would be useful if it actually exists. We may fail to discover what the ancients knew but the hope of success keeps us at our task. With this carrot dangling in front of us we will likely push on whether or not our endeavors lend themselves to literary ends.

Because we have witnessed results from pyramid experiments and because we believe effects of a real though unusual nature occur within pyramid space, we are quite serious about our work. Our primary concern remains to produce sufficient evidence to elicit the interest of trained investigators with skills and facilities superior to our own. We are not interested in promoting pyramids per se. We believe our assignment has been to report the effects as they occur, whatever the outcome, and to not take liberties with the facts. If something fails to work, if some experiment produces zero or negative results, we want to know about it, and we want to pass this information along to others.

We regret that some promoters of pyramid products have taken advantage of public interest to exploit the field for quick monetary gain. It was to be expected but is nonetheless unfortunate. The view is distorted by sensationalism and inflated claims. This caricaturization tends to turn the serious student away. Hopefully, however, people are becoming more sophisticated and able to sort the grain from the chaff. The fact that pyramid research is classified in some people's minds with the occult doesn't particularly disturb us. Though the word "occult" has been badly characterized of late by a considerable array of misleading and erroneous literature, its original meaning had to do with that which is hidden from ordinary view. Along with the stacks of occult fiction passed off as non-fiction there is a considerable body of valuable occult literature going back to ancient times. This tradition bases its findings on knowledge gained through mystical or transcendental states of consciousness. When we begin to realize that all religion is dependent upon these states and that science is now vindicating in many instances the contentions long held by mystics, we recognize that "hidden knowledge" means nothing more than an understanding not accessible through our five senses. A round earth was hidden knowledge at one time, as were bacteria and electricity. Only a few years ago the only people talking about human auras were the mystics. Now Kirlian photogra-

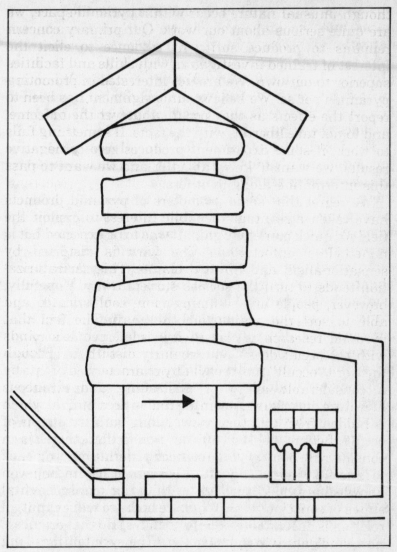

Drawing showing construction of King's Chamber with gabled roof.

phy and sensitive voltmeters have brought the study of auras into the laboratory. If we lean on the original definition of occult, quite a little pyramid experimentation falls into that category, yet no more so than a physicist looking for an unknown particle. When he locates his particle and we find out why a pyramid behaves in the way that it does then that which is hidden becomes the known.

The fact that a pyramid does not always produce a predictable result adds to its mystery but this is probably due less to strange forces at play than it is to the fact that the pyramid reacts in a sensitive fashion to a host of interacting fields. Judging from the results, some of which can be produced by other means, a number of these forces are known, such as electricity, magnetism, radioactivity, etc., of the electromagnetic spectrum. Some phenomena are fairly consistent, such as food preservation and dehydration, but there are results which are difficult to explain, particularly those that come in odd combinations. Exceptions to the rule have a way of disproving theories and our experiences with exceptions led us into another most exciting realm.

When we indulge in descriptions of antimatter, particles which move faster than the speed of light, and negative space-time, the reader might at first imagine that we have joined the ranks of science-fiction writers. Actually, we are keeping company with some of the world's foremost physicists. Einstein led us to believe that nothing could travel faster than the speed of light. Now there are reasons—reasons which we will examine in the following chapter—to believe that there are particles which travel faster than the speed of light to which science has assigned the name of "tachyons." In allowing for the existence of tachyons we can explain certain phenomena which escaped us before. But tachyons behave just the opposite to particles moving at or below the speed of light and this peculiar business prompted scientists, such as Dr. William Tiller of

Stanford University, to speculate that there is not only positive space-time—the world with which we are more or less familiar—but also negative space-time. Negative space-time is one hundred and eighty degrees around from positive space-time. In positive space-time objects are attracted to the center of the earth by what we refer to as gravity; in negative space-time objects are rejected such as in levitation. In positive space-time living organisms change from life to deterioration; but in negative space-time life moves from deterioration to rejuvenation.

This is a different world, one of non-space and where time flows backward, but it may not in any sense be alien to our experiences. It may call, however, for a new level of awareness on our part in order for us to recognize the other face of reality. At that moment of awakening, as some of the world's great teachers have referred to it, we may better understand the Indian occupation with "Prana," or the Chinese reference to "Chi," as universal energy. When we read of the properties of Prana or Chi we are puzzled by descriptions of energy fields which seem to include but also go beyond what we have understood to be the forces of nature. Could it have been that the ancient sages were describing fields on both sides of the fence?

"Let there be light," it is stated in Genesis. Is light the dividing line between two realities? In our positive space-time framework light is the upper limit of existence, but in negative space-time it is the lower level of existence.

Jonathan Livingston Seagull's driving motivation was to fly faster and faster. Whatever his speed it was not good enough. One day he passes beyond the realm of positive space-time, yet finding himself on the other side does not deter him from seeking the absolute in speed. Finally, his teacher says to him, "Perfect speed, my son, is being there..." Space and time as we understand them become meaningless in the dimensions of antimatter.

Light is fast; it moves at the rate of 186,282 miles per second in a vacuum. But it is not fast enough to serve as the carrier wave for thought. Nor will traveling at the speed of light serve our turn in the vast reaches of space, for celestial bodies beyond our own solar system are many light-years away. If we expect to develop any real social exchange with our fellow inhabitants of this universe, we will have to do much better. We won't make many social visits plodding along at the speed of light.

Our adventures with pyramids have taken us down many fascinating and fulfilling paths. None, however, has been more mind-boggling or more important than the realm with which we are confronted in this book. Pyramids took us through the gallery displaying the electromagnetic forces. Some of the faces would be recognized, but we emerged at the far gate with some of our phenomena still in hand and no place to hang them. But the tour didn't end there. We picked up a few clues here and there, sufficient hints for a continued search for a clearer picture of reality, and the research which followed placed us at the threshold of another space and time. In the chapters which follow we will describe experiments which have led us to believe that the results can only be explained by means of the tachyon—that particle which moves faster than the speed of light. We cross the threshold into negative space-time, an exciting outing to say the least. Accepting our findings, what then is the pyramid?

We will propose that the pyramid serves as the interface between positive and negative space-time. It serves as the bridge between matter and antimatter and becomes the gate or the instrument through which two realities meet and interact. Did the ancient builders of the Great Pyramid understand this? Judging from the perfection of their construction and the fact that a slight alteration in their design would have failed to produce the results obtained from its models we have to assume that they did. It is quite likely that we will never be certain about this, but does it really matter? In the final analysis what is of the utmost importance is the knowledge gained whatever the source.

Marveling at the design of the Great Pyramid, there is one factor of its shape which has been overlooked by most scholars and by contemporary experimenters. This has to do with the slight indentation of the sides. We mentioned this fact briefly in our other writings but failed to recognize its great importance in our earlier research. But when we became involved in studies of the angles of light refraction and reflection—particularly with the use of the laser beam—we discovered that this slight alteration in the sides of the pyramid had a great deal to do with the focusing and intensity of energy in key location. Our experiments and those of others have demonstrated that pyramids with flat planes have been effective in producing results. In light of our recent findings—discussed in some detail later—we believe, however, that the indented sides will prove to be superior. We would suggest to those who are seriously involved in pyramid research or who are contemplating the construction of larger pyramids to run some comparison tests before they proceed further.

Recently on a national television program a scientist mentioned that he had placed a razor blade in the King's Chamber of the Great Pyramid and he failed to discover any restoration of the edge. We have not visited with this scientist so we do not know in what manner his experiment was conducted. However, it is quite possible that the Great Pyramid no longer performs in the manner for which it was created. It must be remembered that the finished pyramid had smooth sides but that it was stripped of its veneer more than a thousand years ago to rebuild Cairo following a large earthquake. The Great Pyramid as it now exists has stepped sides and this may make a great deal of difference in its performance as an instrument enhancing or modulating energy. While we have found that one can take certain liberties with the space inside of the pyramid—construction of rooms, etc.—the exterior must remain reasonably smooth to be effective. The reasons for this will be explained further on in the chapters on tachyons and the tracking of light beams. These studies also draw comparisons between open and closed pyramids and discuss the differences. Further, we now have reasons for preferring some materials over others in the construction. This is partly due we feel to the interaction of electromagnetic fields but also to the action of tachyons moving at superluminal speeds.

In light of recent discoveries about pyramid space, the investigation of what is happening to those people now living in pyramid homes is particularly exciting. In our earlier writings we could only speculate as to what their experiences might be. This was fun but the questions were merely academic. But time has passed; people have been living in their pyramid-shaped homes for a sufficient period of time that we can knock on their doors and ask, "What's happening?" We did just that, as a matter of fact, and the readers will find their answers not only fascinating but enlightening. Indeed, we were not disappointed.

Above their interest in changes occurring in solids, liquids, plants, etc., people are particularly engrossed in what happens to people inside of pyramids...not just what changes are involved in their chemistry or electrical systems but to people as living entities in a holistic sense. We now have a considerable body of information on which to report about changes in people living, sleeping, thinking, relaxing, studying, dreaming, meditating, and creating in pyramid space. But of all the experiments we have conducted, the reports we have seen, and the stories we have heard none are more inspiring than the experiences of a mentally retarded girl whose life is no longer the same. Her story is a joyous one and it unfolds on the pages to follow.

So, the research goes on. The field of study gains momentum and its acceleration shows promise of increasing in the foreseeable future. Yet, strangely enough, pyramids remain as great an enigma as ever. If we have learned a few things and our understanding is a little greater than last year or the year before, we are also more aware of the questions still begging answers. But, then, that is the price one pays in searching for greater realities. We feel there is no greater investment.

TWO

Bridge between Worlds

PYRAMID studies have taken us down many strange and wondrous paths. We have been awed, bewildered, enlightened, befuddled, delighted, and frustrated. We have not always been certain what direction to turn, but we have never been bored. We soon learned that although we might not be able to predict the outcome of our experiments, the results, nonetheless, would be worth exploring. Yet, at no time during the past several years have we been more excited about the prospects of what pyramids have to offer than we are at this moment of writing.

This is an ambitious statement, for we have had some fascinating experiences with pyramids as we observed liquids, solids, and plants and people pass through some significant changes under the aegis of pyramid space.

But our research has now carried us to the threshold of time and space and what we will propose on the pages to follow are matters we believe to be of some significance. From the beginning we were aware that pyramids generated, captured, enhanced, channeled, or in some manner made available to objects placed within them an energy flow which was difficult to define.

Some of the results clearly indicated the presence of a force field which could be understood according to the laws of physics. For example, if a plant was stimulated to grow more than a control plant outside of the pyramid, we could hypothesize that this was due to an increase in the magnetic field because this had already been clearly demonstrated by science. What we could then say was that pyramids seem to produce an enriched magnetic environment. This same intensified field could also help explain our findings concerning the healing of tissues and bones. A growing body of medical knowledge points to the speeding up of the healing process within a magnetic and/or electrical field. This will be explored in the chapter on new healing discoveries.

But while some results fell within the domain of the known forces of nature, others defied such classifications. There were frequent occasions when water, for instance, or plants, animals, or humans, seemed to be responding to forces for which there was no reasonable explanation. It was not unusual for something to occur which was exactly opposite from the predictable course of events. Was there some force at play that was opposed to electromagnetic fields or gravity, which behaved one hundred and eighty degrees differently than these known powers? We wondered. Why did water become more purified when exposed to pyramid space and yet take on qualities for which there was no known source of supply? If sealed containers of water gave up some of their mineral content, where did it go? What force was making possible this strange transmutation? If people could get along on less sleep and yet feel more rested by sleeping in pyramids, why would they awaken perhaps several times during the course of the night with vivid dreams rushing through their heads? One would expect them to be so soundly asleep their dreams could not awaken them. Why would a person feel so tranquil in one location of a pyramid and uneasy in another? Why would a solid pyramid outside of and touching the bottom of a fish tank apparently kill the fish while the same pyramid inside of the tank improved their health and vitality?

And so it went. On every hand our experiences were flavored with both the expected and the unexpected. Nor were we always to be sure that two identically conducted experiments would produce identical results. Although some phenomena remained reasonably stable—razor blades continued to be restored, though not always to the same extent; meditation was better inside than outside of a pyramid—the only thing we could be sure of was that things behaved differently inside than outside of pyramids. What factor was present on one occasion and not another? How could this difference be possible? Were we different? Were we part of the circuitry and thus unknowingly affecting the results? Could the differences be attributed to subtle changes in the weather or phases of the moon? Were we dealing with alterations in the electromagnetic fields bombarding us—light, radio, and microwave frequencies, X-rays, gamma rays? We discovered that pyramids are sensitive to sunspot activity. The outcomes of a number of experiments are predictable according to the degree of sunspot activity. This is very important and these findings provide some significant implications. The nature of sunspot activity and its application to pyramid research is discussed in some detail in a later chapter.

But while all of these variables obviously played important roles the fact still remained that some phenomena did not yield to explanation according to the four known forces of nature. These forces had to be discarded as providing the unknown factor, for in many instances they just would not work.

We turned to another world, to another face of reality...of negative space-time, of antimatter. This is the world of the tachyon, those particles which move faster than the speed of light. This is not science-fiction talk. In an age of space travel and monitoring particles infinitely smaller and faster and of galaxies far vaster than we could imagine only a few years ago, it is not uncommon for physicists and mathematicians to speak of realms no longer encompassed by matter as we have always understood it. After considering all the effects and the known energies and faced with phenomena we could not explain with these forces, we were certain an unknown factor was involved. The principal property of the "X" factor was its tremendous speed. It would have some of the characteristics of light but also properties exactly opposite to light. It would have to be faster than light.

But nothing can move faster than the speed of light. This is what we learned in school, taught by no less a teacher than Albert Einstein. Yet if that is true, it means there is a speed limit in nature. The limit is 186,282 miles per second (the velocity of light in a vacuum). Such a limit would prevent us from ever exploring the reaches of the universe, for our nearest neighboring galaxy is 2,250,000 light-years away. A signal from that galaxy would not arrive on earth until 2,250,000 years later. Is there such a speed limit? Why did Einstein conclude that "...velocities greater than that of light have no possibility of existence..."?

Dr. Einstein arrived at this concept in 1905 through his special theory of relativity in order to relate mass and energy, the two basic properties of the universe. He said that $E = mc^2$. ("E" represents energy, "m" is for mass and "c" represents the speed of light.) Any object in motion has mass (the amount of matter) and energy (its capacity to do work). An object's energy varies with its motion, and the faster it travels the more energy it has. If an object's energy increases, its mass must also increase. Why is that? The two sides of the equation—$E = mc^2$—must remain balanced. Therefore, as an object's speed increases, so its mass increases. As mass is a measure of an object's resistance to change of speed, the more massive an object becomes, the harder it is to increase its velocity. Einstein concluded that at the speed of light the mass of an object becomes infinite, and, therefore, nothing can be accelerated to speeds faster than light.

Apparently this is not the end of the story, however. While most scientists continue to agree with Einstein, some of these same scientists are searching for particles which move faster than the speed of light. They have given these particles the name of "tachyons." Particles which move at or slower than the speed of light are known as "tardyons." Are the scientists contradicting themselves? Not necessarily. They explain Einstein's formulas as to mean that nothing can be accelerated beyond the speed of light, but that it may be possible for objects to go faster than light all of the time. Subatomic physics has found that two particles—the "photon" and the "neutrino"—always travel at the speed of light. Is it reasonable, then, to assume that there are particles which always travel faster than light?

Dr. Gerald Feinberg of Columbia University, New York, proposes that the speed of light is a barrier which cannot be crossed. But he adds that there are always two sides to a barrier and that on one side it is possible for particles to exist beyond the speed of light.

Dr. Michael N. Kreisler of the University of Massachusetts proposes that the existence of faster-than-light particles would provide for a balance in nature. This would mean the existence of three classes of particles: particles which travel slower than the speed of light; particles which always travel at the speed of light; and particles which always travel faster than light.

Subluminal and luminal particles are easy enough to find, but how does one go about locating superluminal particles? If tachyons travel faster than other particles, they would arrive at their destination first. It is known that cosmic rays are particles streaking into the earth's atmosphere from somewhere in space. When a cosmic ray particle strikes the upper atmosphere, it produces a group of secondary particles. The secondary particles have been found to travel almost at the speed of light. Drs. Roger Clay and Philip Crouch of the University of Adelaide in Australia, however, propose that some of the particles may be traveling faster than the speed of light. If this is the case, the scientists reasoned, the tachyons would reach the ground slightly ahead of the other particles.

Clay and Crouch developed instruments to check this out. Their devices measure secondary particles produced by cosmic rays, and they established a means to time the impact of the particles. The scientists calculated that the tachyons would strike the detectors about one hundred millionths of a second before the other particles. According to their calculations, some of the particles did arrive ahead of the others and they maintain they have established the existence of tachyons. Other physicists in the world are not so sure and claim that stronger evidence is needed.

Another means of pursuing the elusive tachyon is by means of a photograph of a bubble chamber. A bubble chamber is a container of special liquid, and subatomic particles moving through the liquid leave tiny trails of bubbles. Scientists claim they can identify the particles that pass through the bubble chamber by their trails. They do not expect the tachyons to leave distinct trails but they are hopeful that they may affect the behavior of the particles which do leave trails. So far, however, bubble-chamber studies have failed to produce evidence of tachyons.

We have reasons to believe that some of the unusual phenomena occurring in pyramid space may be the result of tachyons. Our efforts to isolate and describe the energy involved in pyramid phenomena led us to conduct experiments which might rule out particles moving at or below the speed of light as the sole initiators of the results produced. These experiments and the results will be discussed shortly. They are provocative. If we are on the right track in proposing that pyramid energy is partly due to particles moving faster than the speed of light, then the pyramid is an interesting instrument indeed. It has become the bridge between two worlds, the interface between matter and antimatter. If it can serve as the meeting place for positive space-time and negative space-time, the pyramid would not only be the oldest, largest,

Sunflower plant in pyramid. Accented movements west to east on two-hour cycles.

and most mysterious instrument invented by the mind of man, it also would be the most useful. If the ancient builders could put together an instrument in which matter and antimatter could interact, they did indeed have all the energy they could ever need. Some scholars have speculated that the builders could not have possibly constructed the large pyramids by moving the huge boulders into place by primitive methods, but that they had some means of levitating the stone. Other students of the pyramids have claimed that the Great Pyramid, at least, was used to elevate human consciousness to other levels of existence. If the builders could manipulate both positive space-time and negative space-time, then both of the above accomplishments, along with many others, would be possible.

In order to set the stage for the investigation of pyramids and tachyons, however, it would be well for us to review what our experiments revealed and how those led to our explorations in negative space-time. As described in *The Secret Power of Pyramids* and *The Psychic Power of Pyramids,* we found:

1. Sunflower seedlings inside of pyramids grew faster than control plants. The experimental plants gyrated from west to east on approximately two-hour cycles. They

repeated the cycles night and day regardless of the light inside the room.

2. When a small permanent magnet was placed beside the growing plant inside the pyramid, approximately halfway between the roots and the leaves, the lower half of the plant would cease its cyclic movement, while the upper half of the plant continued the gyrations. When the magnet was removed from the pyramid, the entire plant resumed the cyclic movements.

3. When a seedling was placed beneath a Plexiglas half-sphere and then a pyramid placed over the sphere, no cyclic movement of the plant occurred. At the same time, another plant inside the pyramid but not covered by the half-sphere continued limited movements. When a permanent magnet was placed on top of the half-sphere, no change was observed in the plant beneath the half-sphere but the other plant inside the pyramid ceased all movement.

4. When a piece of aluminum foil or screen was placed inside the pyramid on the west side of a growing and gyrating plant, the plant ceased movement and many times growth for several days. Both the cyclic movement and growth resumed when the aluminum was removed.

5. Yet, when the aluminum foil or screen had been placed for a time in a pyramid prior to its being placed on the west side of the plant, the plant continued its gyrations and growth uninhibited.

6. If a piece of untreated aluminum foil or screen was placed between two plants inside a pyramid, the plant to the east of the screen ceased its movement and growth, while the plant to the west of the screen continued both undisturbed.

7. If a piece of aluminum screen or foil was treated for a time inside a pyramid and then placed on the north side of a growing and gyrating plant, the plant ceased its west-east motion and instead moved in a north-south direction.

8. The sunflower seedlings ceased their cyclic movements entirely during the summer of 1974. In the fall of

that year they resumed their gyrations, but the movements began with a north-south pattern and later switched to a west-east gyration. Due to the strange reactions of the sunflowers to aluminum, we made numerous tests with that metal. We found that the aluminum apparently absorbed pyramid energy and could then release it outside of the pyramid. Various food items were wrapped in the treated aluminum and it was found that they were preserved for quite some time without refrigeration.

9. We found that fresh milk when placed inside of a pyramid tended to turn to yogurt within a span of several days, provided there was not a complete lull in sunspot activity. During sunspot lulls the milk reacted as though it had been placed in a container outside of a pyramid, simply stratifying and souring, with resultant mold.

10. Contaminated milk placed within a pyramid would result in the elimination of as much as sixteen percent of the harmful bacteria. An identical sample of milk placed in some other shape of container continued to develop additional bacteria.

11. When well water containing traces of zinc and copper was put in a sealed tube and placed within a pyramid, much of the metal content was removed within fourteen days.

12. Laboratory tests indicated that sodium hydroxide pellets absorbed less water inside the pyramid while control samples placed within other shapes absorbed the usual amount of moisture.

13. According to controlled university tests, plants grown inside of pyramids tended to contain more water than plants grown inside prism- and rectangular-shaped containers.

14. It was found that where abnormalities existed in human blood specimens the blood was brought into normal range when the donor was exposed for a brief period of time to pyramid space.

15. Fruits ripened faster yet remained edible longer

when kept inside a pyramid.

16. There is an apparent freshness and coolness inside a pyramid as compared to the air outside.

17. Healing appears to progress faster and with fewer complications when the subject is subjected to pyramid space.

18. Meditation is reportedly more effective when conducted inside a pyramid.

19. ESP ability is improved while the subject is inside a pyramid.

20. Sleeping inside a pyramid reportedly reduces the length of time required for sleep and the subject is more rested upon arising.

21. Cigarette and pipe smoke dissipates sooner inside a pyramid.

22. Skin temperature, as measured with a GSR (galvanic skin response) device, is increased at the body's extremities while the subject is inside a pyramid.

23. The edges of steel razor blades are restored overnight when placed inside a pyramid.

24. Many drug users have given up drugs after meditating for a length of time inside of pyramids.

25. We have unconfirmed reports that radioactive isotopes decay (lose their radioactivity) faster within a pyramid.

26. Spray paint solvents which fail to accept an electrical charge at the spray nozzle have been found to accept the charge after being exposed to the pyramid shape for a brief period of time.

Whatever the source of the pyramid energy, all the evidence indicated that it was of such a nature that the effect was noticeable only inside the pyramid. Obviously it was not the materials used in the construction of the pyramid. These were not of an unusual nature and when used in some other shape or form no effect was recorded. Pyramid energy, then, was captured, generated, increased, modified, whatever, by the specific shape of the container. Because of our experiences with the plants and the placements of the aluminum screens, which inhibited the growth and movement of the plants, we reasoned that the force must be entering the pyramid from the outside, and for the most part this entrance must be occurring on the west side. The force apparently was able to enter the pyramid without hindrance but was inhibited from leaving the pyramid for some reason.

We were convinced that the aluminum held some clue to the nature of pyramid energy. It above all other metals seemed particularly susceptible to the force. It could so absorb this energy that none was available to the plant and it could retain sufficient amounts that it was able to emit the energy outside of the pyramid.

It was found that a magnetic field inside the pyramid rendered the force ineffective. And any other shape introduced into the pyramid also negated the force.

The more we examined our clues and thought of them in various combinations, the more it appeared to us that the forces with which we were dealing were of a twofold nature: Part of the effects could be defined according to the known forces of nature, but there were other effects which were closely related to that other side of things... negative space-time.

In allowing for the possibility that there is that other side of the universe where things behave in an opposite fashion, the scientists speculate that particles which travel faster than the speed of light—the tachyons—have strange properties. Tardyons, or particles traveling at or below the speed of light, speed up with an increase of energy, yet cannot move faster than the speed of light. Tachyons, on the other hand, slow down with an increase in energy but their speed cannot be reduced to the speed of light. Some scientists believe because of the above properties that tachyons cannot interact with ordinary particles. Stanford University physicist Dr. William A. Tiller, however, has proposed a model of the universe in which there are seven levels of substance. This is basically in agreement with Eastern cosmological systems. The seven levels of substance retain their separate non-interacting identities as far as our five senses or existing measuring devices are concerned. But in actuality, according to this model, the levels are constantly interacting and an activity or disturbance at one level affects all others. Russian studies with mental telepathy have indicated that thought is instantaneous and therefore is traveling faster than the speed of light. This was also demonstrated by former astronaut Edgar Mitchell when on the moon he carried out ESP tests with persons on earth and it was found that telepathic messages took place without a time lag. These tests seem to indicate that thought belongs more to negative than positive space-time.

It has been a question in some people's minds how mind and matter can interact, the one being abstract and the other concrete matter. Yet a thought of worry, fear, anxiety, etc. causes an immediate reaction in the body. Today psychosomatic medicine is concerned solely with the mind's effect on the body. The concept that the mind can both heal and make one ill is acceptable in most medical circles.

Thought has now been measured as an energy field. More accurately, perhaps, we should think of thought producing a vast range of energies, and at one end of its spectrum is a field which is measurable or has a measurable effect on physical substance. According to Indian and Chinese cosmological systems, mind is the interface between physical matter and energies of a less dense nature. This is in agreement with Tiller's model and also that of Dr. H. S. Burr, formerly of Harvard University, who proposed an electrodynamic theory of life in which "life fields" and "thought fields" interact.

The brain is clearly a physical object but the mind is not and many scientists no longer equate the two as being synonymous. More and more the mind is seen as being of a non-physical nature which uses the brain as a piece of equipment. The brain, apparently, serves as an instrument whereby the mind can interact with the physical world. More on these matters later, along with the work of Tiller, Burr, and others, when our attention is focused on healing and some rather fascinating studies with mental disturbance and retardation. But it was necessary to touch base with the unique position that the mind plays in the scheme of things. Science seems to be moving us ever closer to a world in which the basic substratum of life is consciousness rather than atoms and molecules. One of the world's most accomplished scientists, Sir James Jeans, once noted that the more he studied the universe the less it appeared to him to be a gigantic machine than a great thought. And India's great sage Sri Aurobindo explained that it really matters very little whether one considers the basic substance of the universe to be physical, with spirit being its most rarefied form, or whether one chooses to define the universe as spirit, with matter being its most densified form.

When we reflect that our bodies run into all kinds of barriers and restrictions in our environment but that our minds are oblivious to these limitations, we begin to understand how the mind functions in the realm of matter and idea and partakes freely of both positive and negative space-time. We recognize, then, that we are not so unacquainted with antimatter and negative space-time after all. It's just that we have had quite a struggle in getting mind and matter together.

Through the agency of the mind we can understand the interaction between negative and positive space-time. In returning to pyramids with this model in mind, we find ourselves faced with some rather strange paradoxes. The pyramid is clearly a physical object, with all the accompanying properties, and yet it demonstrates qualities which are peculiarly similar to those of the mind. Is it possible that the pyramid can also serve as that bridge between two worlds? Our experiments forced us into that speculation.

We live in a world of opposites. We cannot imagine life

outside of space-time frames of reference. For up there is down, for right there is left, short versus long, black versus white, and so on and on whatever our observations. So theoretically, anyway, it is not so difficult for us to accept that if there are particles which travel below the speed of light, there must also be particles which travel faster than the speed of light; if there is positive space-time, there also exists negative space-time.

Isaac Asimov has stated that theories themselves are nothing but intellectual amusement unless they are supported by observations. Well, we are hard pressed to observe tachyons by our senses or by existing instruments which amplify and expand these senses. The tachyon is just in too great of a hurry to pause for measurements. But knowing the properties of those particles which are more cooperative and aren't so rushed, we can draw some conclusions as to what the properties must be of their opposites. In other words, a tachyon is supposed to behave just the opposite from a tardyon. Then, there are indirect methods of observation through which we can assume the existence of something because of its influence on other things. We needn't find the worm if we have seen the wormhole, and if we see a vapor trail high in the sky, we know there is a plane up there somewhere. This is the position we find ourselves in with the tachyon. Judging from results that are just the opposite from those produced by tardyons, we assume they are created by an opposing force, the tachyon.

How was the tachyon created? Where does it come from? These are as overwhelming as questions such as "What is life?" Nevertheless, we can speculate that tachyons are the offspring of black holes in space, and perhaps of other sources in the universe such as the center of more ordinary stars, like our sun.

A black hole is believed by scientists to form when an entire galaxy collapses, from its own gravitational fields, in upon itself. We might imagine that trillions and trillions of tons of matter are so compressed, so drawn together that the mass is no larger than a peach pit! Astronomers and physicists tell us that the collapsed mass of debris is so dense and the gravitational pull is so intense that not even light can escape from the black hole. The black hole becomes the ultimate in light-absorbent material, an immense vacuum cleaner.

In the process of existing the black hole will draw anything in the vicinity into the blackness where it would be subjected to billions of degrees of heat and untold tons of pressure.

It has been proposed that in the proximity of the black holes, new materials, new particles, and unknown forces would be conceived. These would not necessarily comply with physical laws as we understand them.

Let us imagine, for a moment, a man with such strength in his hands that he can squeeze a watermelon seed to extinction. His strength is such that it would be

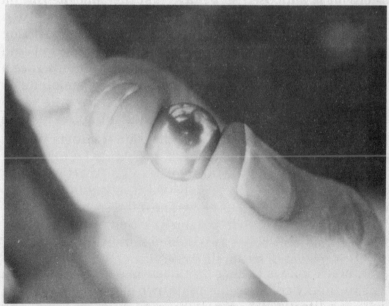

Steel ball between fingers represents the size of the earth if its density was the same as that of a black hole.

extremely difficult for the seeds to escape his grasp. But let's assume that one seed was sufficiently lubricated by juice that instead of being crushed to extinction, it squirted from between his fingers. It might be so mutilated it was no longer recognizable, but it did escape.

Perhaps this can happen to some of the atoms or subatomic particles caught in the squeeze of the black hole. Though they no longer resemble their original selves, they still exist.

Most astronomers and scientists now believe that from the beginning of creation, galaxies have been formed, complete with their suns and planets and the usual debris between. As a galaxy ages, its sun runs out of fuel. The galaxy goes through convulsions and finally collapses upon itself, forming, first a nova (explosion), then the supernova, and ultimately the black hole.

All the particles formerly making up the galaxy are drawn together in a compact mass—still possessing the entire mass and gravity of the galaxy, but now reduced to an infinitesimal point. Some of the particles, the atomic nucleus, may be altered so that they are ejected from the black hole, much as the watermelon seed, but now altered, and now with the ability to travel at no *less* than the speed of light, and possessing other strange characteristics.

Let's picture the tachyon particles now moving from the vicinity of the black hole at such high speeds that they haven't time to interact with the slower atoms of the universe, already in existence.

The tachyons and the tardyons can't interact with one another unless there is a go-between, something which can travel fast as well as slow. The mind seems to fit this bill, as explained earlier, but our question here is whether the pyramid can serve as a common meeting ground.

Since pyramid research came into vogue there have been many exotic claims for the pyramid's power. Some pseudo-scientists have held that there is a strange force collected by the pyramid shape which then shoots out from the apex. But the force flaring from the edges and apex of the pyramid is more than likely high-frequency electricity introduced to the shape to produce a dramatic photograph. The flaring lights visible in such photographs are merely the high voltage "bleeding" into the atmosphere from the sharp point of the apex, much as Ben Franklin demonstrated with his sharp-pointed lightning rods.

The phenomena occurring inside pyramid models cannot be explained by gravity, magnetism, electricity, or light as we know it, although there may be similarities in some cases.

The answer may be found in the properties of the tachyon.

To date there has never been any instrument which can register the existence of pyramid force or energy. Our instruments and training have been directed toward forces in our world, particles which never exceed the speed of light. Now we must rely on observing the influence of tachyons on matter. This can be measured.

Our body of evidence indicates that some force enters the pyramid from the west. This force then seems to become concentrated directly beneath the apex and one third of the distance up from the base to the apex.

Let us assume that the tachyon, ever in motion, is passing through outer space. Its flight from one edge of the universe to the other may take only one billionth of a second, providing that the little particle carries a small enough charge of energy (whatever type of energy tachyons utilize).

The tachyon penetrates stars, suns, rock, metal, liquids, and the sides of pyramids, regardless of their composition. The tachyon passes through organic materials—plastic, plywood, whatever—that may cover the sides of the experimental pyramids. In passing through the lattice of atoms of, say, plywood material, let's assume that the tachyon grabs sufficient energy from the material's atomic makeup so as to cause it to slow down to nearly the speed of light.* At this slower speed the tachyon may have the ability to react somewhat like photons (particles moving at the speed of light).

When slowed somewhat, would the tachyon take on some of the characteristics of the photon?

When a photon (in a beam of light) strikes a plate of glass it is reflected at the same angle at which it struck the glass. Would the tachyon behave in the same manner? Or would it bounce off at a different angle? Would it have different angles of reflection according to the materials which it had passed through on the way to the glass?

When a photon enters a different medium than that through which it has been traveling, it will immediately change speed. If it passes from air to glass, it will slow down, and the angle at which it entered the glass will change as it travels through the glass; at the same time its speed will slow as much as one third, according to the material. This is known as refraction.

But as the photon emerges from the glass into air again it will immediately assume the maximum speed.

Does the tachyon observe the same rules?

Does the tachyon change its angle of travel as it enters another material?

And, if so, what is the change in the angle of refraction?

The tachyon appears to have the quality of changing speed depending on the amount of energy it collects on the way, according to the makeup of the material through which it has passed on the way.

Now, does the tachyon actually change speed, and if so

---

* We have evidence that certain materials placed inside the pyramid actually lose or gain weight (or mass) according to the placement in the pyramid—which perhaps indicates that the energy obtained by the tachyon may well be derived from the energy from the proton of the nucleus of the atom—in turn resulting in a gain in weight, or a loss—depending upon whether the material is in the King's Chamber or beneath the pyramid.

how much? If a change in speed is effected what change would this have on its other properties?

To understand the strange ability of the photon to slow down as it passes through a material and then resumes its original speed as it emerges it may help if you will imagine the photon as a car. Its 100 horsepower motor is connected directly to the four wheels and it clips along at a steady pace of one hundred miles per hour. It must travel at that speed on a dry surface, for the motor will not slow in its revolutions.

It travels along a dry concrete road until it comes to a curve, but it fails to make the curve and lurches into a wet cornfield where the ground is muddy and slick. Although the wheels are still turning at the same rate, the car is slowed to ninety miles per hour because of the mud and the resistance of the tall and thick cornstalks.

The car then runs out of the cornfield and again is on a dry concrete road, the tires grip the surface, and the car increases in speed to one hundred miles per hour. (The car has the same applied energy as it travels through the cornfield as it did on the road, but the resistance of the mud and thick cornstalks has slowed it until it emerges.)

Now let us imagine a tachyon car. This car picks up or loses energy according to the terrain over which it is passing. This vehicle travels faster with a decrease in energy and it travels slower with an increase in energy.

This is a steam-driven car. It has a place at the rear for a man to stand and he feeds the boiler by picking off branches from trees as he passes.

The boiler is immense, requiring tons of fuel to operate the car. But the weight of the fuel in the boiler prevents the car from traveling at any but a slow rate of speed.

However, when the forest thins out and the fuel is consumed in the boiler, the weight is reduced and the car speeds up, since only a bed of light coals remains.

Perhaps the tachyon can actually interact with electromagnetic forces within our universe, and who can say that the tachyon does not draw some type of energy from the nucleus, the electrons, or other parts of the atoms through which it passes?

In passing through the first molecules of the organic material of the pyramid the tachyon may somehow be able to obtain sufficient energy, probably from the proton of the nucleus, or something akin to electricity, or the spinning electrons, or whatever, so that it will slow down controlled by the makeup of the material.

The tachyon thus is slowed to a speed just about that of light and suddenly has the ability to react in some ways similar to the photon.

The tachyon strikes the inside wall of the pyramid, bounces off, and strikes the floor, then on to a point on the opposing wall, and the cycle is repeated until finally, due to the particular angle of the pyramid's sides, the tachyon passes out at a point about one third up from the base to the apex.

However, the force is not centralized or concentrated as we would like in the King's Chamber area. Rather it seems to bounce directly back and forth in line with the point at which it entered.

We need a large enough flow of tachyons to virtually flood the King's Chamber area. But we do not find this concentration; the forces are concentrated, yes, but evenly dispersed from wall to wall, even though the force is somewhat centralized one third up from base to apex.

This perhaps can explain why some experimenters obtain faster growth in their models in one area than another spot. Now, we can attribute this to the fact that, for instance, the plastic sides of the model sag slightly, or the inside surface of the walls is not perfectly smooth, this throwing the force off from its desired path.

Here we make note of a very important fact. The sides of the Great Pyramid, after which all experimental pyramids are modeled, are not flat planes!

Each of the four sides is slightly indented.

This fact went unnoticed for many centuries. Even though Napoleon's engraver depicted the indented sides, the information was ignored until the 1880s, when William Flinders Petrie, an English engineer, determined that the sides were, in fact, indented some thirty-seven inches from a straight line!

Petrie's meticulous measurements were confirmed when a Royal Air Force pilot took an aerial photograph of the pyramid and the shadows clearly revealed the indentations. Peter Tomkins includes this information in his book *Secrets of the Great Pyramid*. Although this book was widely read, the indentation of the sides was overlooked and to this date has not been a factor in experiments with pyramid models.

Our efforts to chart the course of energy fields within the pyramid led us to discover that the indentations in the sides played an all-important role in focusing energy in the center of the pyramid, and particularly in the area of the King's Chamber.

Prior to our experiments with the light beams we envisioned that a ray of light entering the pyramid would strike the opposite wall, be reflected to the floor, bounce back to the wall through which it had entered, and so on. We assumed that the ray of light, due to the sloping walls of the pyramid, would likely converge at a level approximately one third of the distance from the base to the apex.

We conducted experiments with a silvered-glass pyramid. The silver was removed from a spot on the side of the pyramid and a ray of light from a 35-mm projector was directed inside the pyramid, but it was found that unless the light beam was directly in line with the King's Chamber it soon became lost, due to the scattering of the light.

In our previous writings we had mentioned that the sides of the Great Pyramid were indented, but all of our experimental pyramids up to this point were made with straight sides.

We decided to try light reflections with indented pyramids, and we purchased a laser machine (which emits an intense beam of non-scattering light). At the

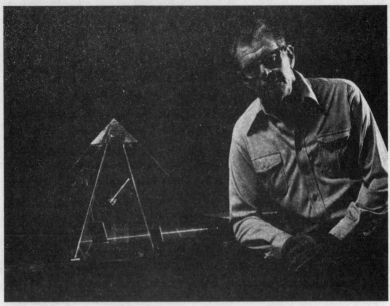

Ed Pettit with twenty-nine-inch glass pyramid with indented sides and solid capstone. Two laser beams encounter King's Chamber area.

same time we obtained many front-surfaced mirrors, so made that the light would be reflected from the surface of the reflective surface, rather than being forced to travel through the glass to the mirrored surface. This prevents much scattering of the light, and enables the beam to be reflected many more times than if conventional mirrors had been used.

A pyramid was constructed of single-strength window glass. Eight pieces of glass were used instead of the usual four triangles in order to indent the sides. Each triangular side was divided from the apex to the center of the base, thus producing eight identical pieces. A clear silicon seal material was used to fasten the pieces together, forming a flexible hinge at each junction.

Once the pyramid was formed, the sides could be indented to the desired angle simply by slipping some shims under each of the corners. The evenly elevated corners caused a sagging of the four sides at the base, resulting in the sides being indented slightly. Now we had a pyramid with slightly concave sides.

Anyone wishing to experiment with light beams can construct a pyramid with ordinary mirrored glass. Four identical sides should be made, or eight pieces (each piece would be one half of a side), if one plans to try the indented pyramid.

The pyramid should be then set upon a mirror the size of the base or larger. One or more openings can be made by scratching off a small amount of the silver backing. A flashlight beam can be used to shine through one of the openings.

A fine wire can be used to suspend a small piece of white plastic at the level of the King's Chamber. The beam of light *must* enter the pyramid *from the horizontal.* Our tests indicate that the force enters the pyramid precisely on the horizontal, and parallel to the base of the pyramid.

The laser beam was shone through the side of our clear glass pyramid. At each point where the beam struck a wall or base inside the pyramid we attached a small front-surface mirror to reflect the beam.

As mentioned, we used the clear glass pyramid so as to observe and photograph the beam as it was directed throughout the pyramid, and by means of the front-surface mirrors we were able to observe the beam for a greater number of reflections. If the model pyramid is of mirror stock, the light beam will be diffused after only a few reflections due to the scattering each time it is forced to travel through the clear glass to the silvered backing.

We made the pattern for the glass pieces so that when the pyramid was assembled the top four inches of the pyramid would be missing. In this way we could reach inside to apply the mirrors and also this gave us the opportunity to place various capstones on the pyramid.

We were elated when we directed the laser into the pyramid and placed the mirrors and then found that in nearly all cases, when a plastic King's Chamber was placed in the appropriate spot it would light up with an intense red glare as the beam crossed that area.

Even a slight alteration of the elevation of the sides would minimize the effect. (It appears that the indentations will cause the beam to be thrown off course, so that only by experimentation can the optimum amount of indentation be obtained.)

In our first successful tests we used a pyramid with a thirty-inch base, and elevated the sides some seven sixty-fourths of an inch.

We can assume that with no loss of the beam, if we could follow the beam as the tachyon would travel, there would be a continual crossing of the King's Chamber area resulting in an intense concentration in that area.

Another curious thing was noted. Those beams that did not enter the King's Chamber area directly would always complete their cycle by striking the exact junction of the flat planes where they were joined together.

We shall go further with our conjectures in subsequent chapters but it may be well to speculate that in the indented pyramid we perhaps have a positive and negative flow of energy. Let's say that the King's Chamber is the positive side and the junctures of the flat planes, the corners, and the indented areas of the sides give the negative side of the force.

From our first pyramid experiments several years ago it was found that the best location for producing maximum results was usually the location of the King's Chamber. Since sufficiently sensitive instruments were not available for measuring the energy field, it was not possible to demonstrate by any direct means that this particular location was actually the best.

Nor was it possible, outside of pointing to results, to claim that an experimental pyramid should have the exact proportions of the Great Pyramid, and that errors in the construction could inhibit the results.

But now, looking at the ruby-red beam as it constructed

geometrical figures inside the pyramid and converged in the center at one third of the distance from base to apex, we experienced the elation of providing scientific proof for a long-held hypothesis.

In *The Secret Power of Pyramids* and *The Psychic Power of Pyramids* we did not stress great accuracy in the construction of pyramid models as it was found that models with minor errors still sharpened razor blades and dehydrated eggs. But working with the laser beam we soon learned the need for precision.

First, we built a base for the laser unit that had roller-bearing slides and thus allowed us to traverse the side of the pyramid without throwing the laser off the level plane. This was much more satisfactory than trying to hold the machine level.

When we used this procedure, an accurately construct-ed pyramid produced a concentration of light in the King's Chamber, but even small errors in construction, leveling of the base, elevations of the corners, and so on would result in less than perfect results.

Undoubtedly, experimentation with straight-sided pyramids, constructed only to an approximation of the Great Pyramid, will continue to yield fascinating results. However, the laser experiments indicate that finally there is a need for precision as industry and serious researchers enter the field.

Witnessing the phenomena of light concentration in the King's Chamber and the remainder impinging on the intersections of the flat planes we were once again reminded of the ancient builders of the Great Pyramid. Clearly they knew exactly what they were doing with their designs and in some manner determined that the sides had to be indented to produce desired results.

If they wished to leave a body of knowledge to mankind, how better than to use an enduring shape made of stone, the universal material, virtually indestructible. It would be so constructed that it would continue to arouse interest through the ages but would be of such a complex nature that its secrets could be unraveled only by an advanced civilization.

In the meantime, certain mathematical information would be incorporated, such as the base perimeter divided by the height yielding the universal constant of pi, and much more information involving geometry and the Universe. The builders knew that this information would be noted and an intense interest in the structure throughout the world would thereby be retained. To further the speculation, part of the interior would be so designed as to cause at least some of the changes brought about by the shape alone. To bring about such physical changes such as dehydration and so forth the builders incorporated in the King's Chamber such materials as would bring about subtle but noticeable alterations. How better to do this than to construct the King's Chamber of a piezoelectrical material? (Certain materials, such as the quartz-bearing granite used in the King's Chamber, subjected to a mechanical stress—that is, a pressure or tension—applied to opposite faces will produce a measurable flow or emission of electricity.)

Certainly the builders knew that there would be tremendous pressures brought to bear upon the immense granite walls of the chamber, and certainly such gigantic pressures would create an intense electrical field within the chamber.

Modern scientists are aware of the fact that electrical fields, and magnetic fields, are beneficial to man when properly applied. And who can say that the electrical field generated by the enclosure of the King's Chamber would not bring about dramatic changes in a body, living or otherwise, inside the chamber?

When the material (granite) was newly installed there would likely have been strange properties indeed noted in this chamber. Even now, after untold centuries of pressure, there are still dramatic changes noted within the chamber, such as the dehydration and preservation of animal bodies, changes in living creatures who spend even so short a time as overnight inside the chamber, and who can say what the effects might have been when the chamber's materials were "fresh"?

We shall go into further detail later in the book as regards the differences in such a chamber and the space inside the pyramid model which utilizes only the shape, without the filling stone, of the Great Pyramid.

But why the indented sides? How better to focus the forces entering the pyramid model from the west than by indenting the sides slightly? In this manner, tachyons (energy), wherever they entered, which actually would be the entire west side of the pyramid, would strike the opposite side and be "reflected" to the base of the pyramid, thence to the north side, on to the south side, and, providing the indentation was correct, most would enter the King's Chamber. Depending upon the area they entered on the west side, additional reflections might occur before they encountered the King's Chamber, but in our experience no more than seven reflections seem to be needed to accomplish this.

Now, to consider a basic question.

Let us assume that the tachyon was designed to be of use in growing and evolving life on this or another planet. In such a case the tachyon must travel at a *slow* rate of speed, although still *faster* than light, and it seeks energy to keep it at such a slow pace. It would be ineffective at its highest speeds, thus the need for the built-in energy hunger.

What better source of energy than magnetism, cosmic rays, atomic nuclei, all of which can be found in the solar wind? The solar wind speeds from the sun bearing known and unknown particles. As the solar wind nears the earth it is caught up in the planet's magnetism and is whipped about the earth by its rotation. The tachyons, seeking energy, head for the solar wind and by the time they have whipped about the earth they have consumed a great deal of energy. They have been slowed by this process and can interact with slower particles, but, remember, there is still no tachyon concentration.

As early as 1900 the nuclear physicists were studying the manner in which radiation from radioactive substances knocked electrons out of atoms in the atmosphere, leaving in its path atmospheric atoms with a deficiency of electrons which they termed positive ions. These atoms carried what was known as a positive charge.

It was then found that samples of air, even when enclosed in lead containers, would somehow or other accumulate a small number of positive ions. Something was penetrating the lead sheathing! The "something" would strike an atom in the air, displace an electron, and thus form a positive ion.

Extensive tests eliminated the soil of the earth as the source for these unknown particles, but it was found by sending instruments into the higher reaches of the atmosphere that the higher the instruments the more of the highly energetic particles were encountered. Scientists called this high-altitude radiation at first, but later the particles were known as "cosmic rays" because they seemed to originate in outer space.

Extensive tests were made to identify the particles in the 1920s. At that time all the massive particles known possessed a positive charge of electricity, and the scientists wondered if the cosmic rays possessed an electric charge, and if so, was the charge positive or negative?

It was found that cosmic rays approached the earth from all directions. So, the scientists reasoned, if the particles carry a positive charge, they would be deflected by the magnetic poles of the earth and the lines of magnetic force surrounding the earth. Therefore, there would be a higher concentration at the polar regions, near the magnetic poles, than elsewhere.

If, on the other hand, the particles were photons, they would possess no electrical charge and would be unaffected by the magnetism. There would be an equal fallout of the particles on every spot on earth.

In the 1930s it was clearly demonstrated that the particles were more concentrated in the polar regions than elsewhere. Physicist Bruno Rossi explained that the deflection of the rays would vary according to whether the charge was positive or negative. Positively charged particles would be deflected so that they would appear to be approaching more from the west than any other direction, and this proved to be the case.

This appears to explain why the forces concentrated in the pyramid shape appear to be entering predominantly from the west. This might also explain why the builders of the Great Pyramid located the structure on the edge of the Libyan Desert with its desolate reaches to the west. There would be no obstruction to the path of the tachyons, which follow the energetic particles of the cosmic rays and the solar winds created by solar flares.

What is known as the photoelectric effect offers convincing proof that photons of light can transfer energy to electrons. If the photons of light can transfer energy to electrons in the photoelectric cell, we believe that we can assume that the tachyon, when suitably controlled, can transfer energy to electrons in a similar metal or other substances, and thus produce a usable flow of electricity.

Einstein in 1905 assumed that light is a stream of energy particles that he called photons. Einstein's photons were not minute bits of matter, as had been thought in the past. Rather they were particles of energy that acted like matter!

The greater the number of photons emitted from, for instance, a heated wire which produced visible light, the shorter the intervals at which they would leave and the heavier the impact they would have upon striking a material. The number ejected from the heated wire per given length of time is known as the frequency.

To give a better picture of frequency, imagine a rifle which can shoot bullets at such high speed that during high-speed firing perhaps several bullets will be in the barrel at one time, each following the one in front closely. If the bullets were counted for, say, one second as they emerged from the muzzle of the gun, we would have the frequency. Perhaps one hundred per second.

In 1923 an American physicist, Arthur H. Compton, noted that when a beam of X-rays (X-rays have a very high frequency) was passed through a gas some of the X-rays would be scattered. The scattered X-rays were found to have a lower frequency than the original beam. Compton found that the X-rays, in passing through the gas, would collide with electrons in the gas and bounce off. In the process the X-rays gave some of their energy to the electron with which they collided, and the X-rays thereby lost some of their velocity.

Now, let us assume that the tachyon has some properties just the opposite to photons. We know that the photon loses energy upon contact with an electron. We believe that the tachyon gains energy upon contact, either with electrons or the nucleus (proton) perhaps in the atom's interior. As the tachyon gains energy it will slow—exactly opposite to other electromagnetic radiation, which speeds with an increase of energy.

We believe that the tachyon behaves somewhat in the above manner.

As it encounters the atoms in the material making up the walls of the pyramid, the tachyon would gain energy and slow its speed. With each collision with the sides or base of the pyramid it would be slowed further until it was able to interact with materials inside the pyramid.

Depending upon the molecular makeup of the material in the wall of the pyramid the tachyon would slow more or less. Perhaps some particular material or combination of materials will cause it to immediately slow to acceptable levels, while if the walls are of other materials we believe that two or more reflections will be needed to bring this about.

Now, since the tachyon's speed depends upon the type of material through which it passes, what happens in the case of aluminum, for instance?

We mentioned earlier our experiments in which aluminum screen or foil, when placed to the west of a growing plant in the pyramid, inhibited (or stopped) the growth and normal movement of the plants. Other metals proved to affect the behavior of the plants, but to a lesser extent.

We know that aluminum is one of the most abundant metals in the earth. It is different than most other metals in that it retains its metallic and silvery shine. In *Of Matters Great and Small,* Isaac Asimov explains that "as soon as the metal is formed, the aluminum atoms on the surface bind themselves strongly to oxygen atoms in the air. The aluminum oxide thus formed remains on the surface, one molecule thick, and forms so tight and coherent a layer that the aluminum atoms underneath aren't touched by additional oxygen even over a prolonged period."

Perhaps it is this combination of oxides and the aluminum that causes the metal to take energy from the tachyon as it passes through. The sudden decrease in energy causes the tachyon to immediately take flight, perhaps at many times the speed of light, and the great velocity causes it to speed on through the wall of the pyramid, never pausing to interact with anything inside the pyramid.

Let's pause here for another mental picture. We are inside a pyramid, we have a round steel ball. We throw the ball at the side of the pyramid; it does not have sufficient "force" to penetrate the wall of the pyramid and merely bounces off. It has a slow velocity. Let's pick up the ball and load a gun and place the ball in the barrel and fire the gun. The ball now has sufficient force, or energy

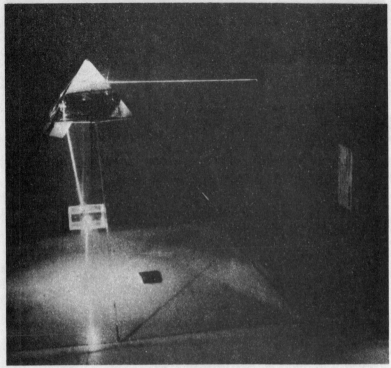

Beam from laser enters solid capstone and is directed down and through King's Chamber.

(velocity), so as to go right on through the wall of the pyramid.

At the same time that the tachyon possesses such an amount of energy that it can penetrate the pyramid side, its velocity will prevent it from being able to interact with plant cells, which causes the cessation of movement and growth in the plant—providing, that is, that the tachyon is actually the regulator of living cells and therefore life as we know it.

Let's see now if we can gain another clue as to the presence of tachyons by considering plants placed in pyramids. Georges Lakhovsky stated a number of years ago that "All cells capable of reproduction contain in their nuclei 'filaments' of highly conductive material surrounded by insulating media...This filament, which may be the RNA-DNA complex, is always in the form of a spiral or helix, in other words, a coil. Therefore, each will react as a tuned circuit if its resonant frequency can be approximated by an external oscillation."

Now, consider that the RNA complex actually has been found to be a spiral or helix, but for comparison we shall picture a piano string—as the other strings are played, one or another of them will cause the first string to vibrate and this string will be found to have a resonant frequency which causes the string in question to vibrate at its assigned frequency.

The tachyon can operate in a similar manner. As it penetrates the cell wall of the cell, it will be regulated so that its speed will cause the helix to vibrate at exactly the desired frequency, in turn causing it to operate at maximum efficiency.

Let's assume that the seedling, with the usual cellular material making up the slender stem, is placed inside a pyramid shape. Let us say that the pyramid sides are cardboard. It is therefore organic, or made up of materials which were formerly living plants or creatures.

The stem of the plant is composed of many, many cells, the interior ones capable of dividing and reproducing, while the outer shell of the stem is composed of cells which, while they may not divide, tend to elongate and become larger in general. The DNA molecule transfers the information as to the exact makeup of the cell that is to be duplicated to the RNA molecule in the nucleus of the cell and then the RNA can supervise the exact cellular makeup. Due to the information in the RNA, the reproduced cell will be exactly like the mother cell. But we must remember that any damage to the mother cell will be reproduced in the daughter cell.

We might say that such damage is hereditary. We might compare this to a human mother who had a broken leg. Then her daughter would of necessity be born with a broken leg. Of course, this is not the case as far as the complete organism is concerned. Certain inherent weaknesses may be passed on to the daughter of the human, but not all damage is thus transferred.

In the cell, however, the damage to the RNA must of necessity be passed on to the daughter cell.

But all is not lost, perhaps. Let's assume that one connecting strand is broken—a strand that may connect two parts of the RNA together, and when duplication is completed, then the newly formed cell would have a broken strand unless, that is, the broken strand could be re-formed.

We feel that this can in fact be done, to a certain extent by the passage of properly directed tachyons. As the tachyon speeds through the cell and the RNA begins to vibrate at its assigned frequency, then perhaps the break would automatically be repaired, resulting in a perfect daughter cell.

Let's assume that it is the passage of the tachyons which is the prime factor in cell division in plants, animals, and man. Further, let's assume that life cannot exist without tachyon regulation.

Inside the pyramid the tachyon flow from the west will naturally strike more cells on the west side, since the particles enter from the west. The cells will grow longer and divide at a faster rate on that side, causing the plants to bend to the east. As the plant reaches nearly a horizontal position the tachyon flow passes over the plant, strikes the opposite side of the pyramid, reflects from the floor, and strikes the cells on the east side of the stem. The cells inside the stem grow faster, while the stem wall cells elongate and the plant bends to an upright stance and then on to the west again.

We described in *The Secret Power of Pyramids* the experiments with the aluminum screen. We found that when a piece of aluminum screen is placed vertically on the west side of a growing sunflower plant, so that the stem is shielded from the tachyon flow, the metal will apparently absorb the energy entering the pyramid.

At the time we did not have sufficient data to determine the source or the nature of the energy being utilized by the plant, but we now feel that the energy is the tachyon flow.

As mentioned earlier, in traversing the atoms of the metal the tachyon gives up energy to the metal atoms, resulting in a dramatic speeding of the tachyon, thus causing it to penetrate the outer walls of the pyramid, and because of its speed it is unable to interact with the plant's cells. In other words, the plant is no longer subjected to the flow of the tachyon life force and will not grow.

It is commonly known that an aluminum pan placed on a fire will get hot and that the heating of the metal is caused by a transfer of heat energy to the metal. This heating causes the molecules of the aluminum to vibrate or move faster, thus causing the heating effect. As the pan

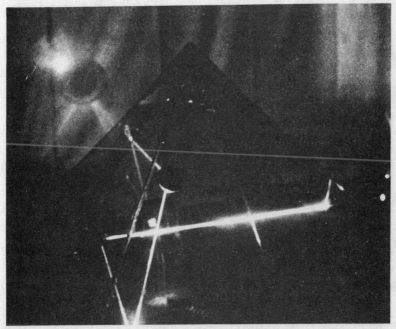

Laser tracing in pyramid.

cools, the molecules slow down in their frantic movement until the pan reaches room temperature. We might bear this in mind when we think of the aluminum inside the pyramid being subjected to a concentration of tachyon energy. If this energy, instead, was of the tardyon world, the metal would heat up as the molecules increased their vibratory rate and the temperature of the metal would rise.

Despite an apparent concentration of energy in the metal, however, the temperature does not rise, neither in the metal nor in the air. That is, the thermometer will not show a change.

If a ray of light—such as sunlight—is allowed to shine into a pyramid, the temperature rises. On the other hand, if we introduce a beam of tachyon energy (a negative energy) into the pyramid, while the temperature does not rise—as measured by our instruments—a sense of "coolness" is experienced by virtually everyone who has gone into the pyramid for the first time. We believe that this feeling of coolness is caused by the flow of tachyons. While the body does not register a rise in temperature, as such there is a sense of change. The coolness and freshness of the air are reported by persons from all parts of the earth. And we repeatedly receive reports that there is a noticeable lack of odor in the pyramid.

Ultraviolet light has long been used to purify air, to reduce bacterial growth, resulting in a better preservation of foodstuffs. Does the tachyon behave in some fashion similar to ultraviolet light? After all, we have speculated that the tachyon will be found to be in the area below the known electromagnetic spectrum well below ultraviolet light.

We believe that here again we have evidence that such occurrences relate directly to the tachyon and its regulation within the pyramid shape.

During the compilation of this part of the book we noticed an Associated Press release, dateline January 3, 1978. We were quite elated when we noted that the article stated that scientists plan to send twenty sunflower plants into space during the 1980 U.S.-European Spacelab mission so that their growth and movements can be monitored by time-lapse movies. The purpose of this experiment is to attempt to determine why the sunflower plant "wiggles."

They noticed that the tip of the growing plant moved slightly in a helix or spiral, making one revolution in about one hundred minutes. They have attributed this to the effect of gravity and reason that if the effect is caused by gravity, in the gravity-free Spacelab there will be some difference noted.

On page 63 of *The Secret Power of Pyramids* we outline our experiments with sunflower plants, and their strange antics inside a pyramid shape. We note, "We wondered if this effect could be observed by the use of time-lapse photography." What we saw—and subsequently showed to a number of scientific and lay observers—were plants gyrating in a symphonic dance as though led by an unseen conductor.

Our first film showed a sunflower approximately six inches tall, slender, with two well-formed leaves, placed at the center of a glass pyramid at the level of the King's Chamber, one third the distance from the base to the apex. The plant followed an east-west cyclic movement. It bowed to the east nearly touching the base, swept a semicircle to the south and back to the west, and finally straightened to the vertical before starting the dance once more. The movement was repeated every two hours, according to a clock placed beside the plant. Time-lapse photography has since been used a number of times over a period of two years.

We go on, in the same book, to outline our search to determine the cause of the movements, and the cause of the cessation of movement in the summer of 1974. We finally traced the movement to sunspot activity with perhaps the assistance of earth magnetism.

In the newspaper article mentioned, Dr. Allan H.

Brown, a plant pathologist at the University of Pennsylvania, says, "The tip of the elongating shoot moves in a helix—besides being a very tiny motion, it happens slowly." He goes on to say that science has speculated that this movement is either natural for the plant or caused by earth's gravity.

Certainly the plant movement in the pyramid shape during sunspot activity is anything but a "tiny" movement.

At this point we would like to speculate on the results of the plant experiment as observed by the camera in the Spacelab during the 1980 test.

But first we must recapitulate: We have mentioned that aluminum appears to absorb tachyon energy, causing it to be ineffective in its control over cells of living things.

However, it seems that when the aluminum metal has been exposed to a concentration of tachyons for a sufficient length of time, the inhibiting effect is overcome and the aluminum then has the property of "giving off" tachyon energy, whether it is in the pyramid or outside.

After the aluminum screen has been inside a pyramid for a length of time it no longer hinders the tachyon flow and the plant's movements are no longer altered by a screen near the plant.

So here we have a problem in predicting the effect of space on a growing sunflower plant.

The first unknown is: Has the aluminum shell of the spacecraft been subjected to the tachyon flow sufficiently so that it will no longer act as a shield? If not, we predict that the sunflowers will show a marked decrease in the movements, or a cessation altogether. We have no idea as to the concentration of tachyons in space. Perhaps the flow will be much heavier than on earth. Perhaps not. We believe that such tests will reveal that gravity has no bearing on the tests, but we do feel that the absence of a magnetic field will definitely have a bearing on the results. Which leads us to urge that in some of the tests an artificial magnetic field be provided for the plants.

We believe that the plants will show a greater movement when placed near a porthole, and that the movements will increase as the rotating Spacelab faces this port toward the sun.

Of course, a botanist will say that of course the plant will grow better in the rays of the sun. However, in our experience the lack of sunlight made no difference in the amplitude of the movements of the sunflowers. All our tests were conducted in a darkened frame building: Only the light which allowed the picture to be taken disturbed the darkness. To make sure that the light was not a factor we altered the timing from one frame each three minutes to one per four minutes and one per five minutes. None of this alteration of light sequence seemed to change the time of the cycles or the growth of the plants.

During the tests the Spacelab will be monitoring the sun for all types of activity. It will be well for the scientists to correlate sunspot activity and solar magnetism to the plant movements.

Of course we would like to see tests similar to ours made on sunflower plants. Sunflower activities inside a pyramid shape on earth would be compared to the plants' activities in the same pyramids in space.

There is another unknown variable. The Spacelab, in addition to being surrounded by the inhibiting aluminum, will have miles of wiring, artificial lighting, running motors, and the like which will cause the tests to be somewhat confusing when it comes to pinpointing the causes of any changes noted.

There is a chance that between the time this book is published and the time of the Spacelab tests we will have a sufficient amount of data as regards the tachyon, and its effects on matter, that the results of the tests can be readily predicted.

A magnetic field, even one of moderate strength, apparently renders the tachyon ineffective in the pyramid. We believe that the magnetic field absorbs energy from the tachyon, as does the metal.

Laser beam refracted and reflected down to gabled roof over King's Chamber, then reflected to side of pyramid.

It would seem that the field surrounding the magnet strengthens the magnetic field of the earth. This being the case, a portion of the area near the floor of the pyramid would carry sufficient strength to absorb tachyon energy so that virtually all of the tachyons entering below the level of the magnet would speed on out of the pyramid. On the other hand, the tachyons in the upper part would be free to rebound, would penetrate the stem cells and thereby affect their growth.

It is our belief that future research will demonstrate that there are radical enough changes in the earth's magnetism that even points a few miles apart will have a wide variance in field strength. This would help explain reported differences in experimental results with persons in the same city and done at the same time.

It is known that sunspots have intense magnetic fields. Sunspots have been known since the time of Galileo. They appear to travel across the sun from east to west and rotate on a cycle of approximately twenty-seven days. According to James H. Nelson, Louis Hurwitz, and David G. Knapp, authors of *The Earth's Magnetism*, a publication of the U. S. Department of Commerce, sunspots vary in size but may have diameters of 50,000 kilometers or more. Probably the largest sunspot on record was seen in 1958, with a diameter of 230,000 kilometers (eighteen times the diameter of the earth!).

Sunspot activity varies over the years and careful monitoring has revealed a cycle that averages out to slightly more than eleven years. This is mentioned because we have found a link between sunspot activity and pyramid phenomena.

In recent years scientists have learned that the weather on earth is largely determined by the amount of sunspot activity. During years of high sunspot activity (and high tachyon flow, in our opinion) there is ample rainfall and summers are not so severe and there are high crop yields.

During the years of minimum sunspot activity (and decrease in tachyons) droughts occur, summers are unusually hot, and crops suffer. Stephen Schneider of the National Center for Atmospheric Research in Boulder, Colorado, and Clifford Mass of the University of Washington, Seattle, reported finding a statistical correlation between sunspot activity and worldwide surface temperatures. Dr. Louis M. Thomson, associate dean of agriculture at Iowa State University, has been saying for quite some time that droughts occur during years of least sunspot activity.

Sunspots may occur singly or in groups, but they are often noted in pairs with opposing magnetic polarity. As the sunspots are fields of intense radiation, they determine the amount of solar radiation reaching the earth on the solar wind. If some tachyons are produced in the sun this would account for an increase in concentration, and if they actually derive energy from the radiation and actually do whip around the earth, this would account for the increase in growth and well-being for the inhabitants of this planet.

In our mode of thinking, then, a decrease in solar activity will result in the pyramid being less effective for many purposes.

Prior to our interest in tachyons and sunspot activity we ran into a perplexing problem. We had been running time-lapse photography of plant behavior within pyramid space for more than two years. During this time our sunflowers housed within pyramids outdid the controls in growth rate as they danced through their west-east two-hour cycles. But suddenly during the summer of 1974 the plants stopped their gyrations. We were at a loss as to why. We checked the pyramids to see if they were still in correct alignment. Finding that they were, we wondered if the plants' limbo could be attributed to increases in some electromagnetic fields, radio waves, microwaves, etc. in our area. Nothing. Finally we turned to the National Geophysical and Solar-Terrestrial Data Center in Boulder, Colorado, hoping that they could tell us something about shifts in the earth's magnetic fields, or give us some appropriate clues.

Through this agency's charts we learned that sunspot activity was then nearing the bottom of an eleven-year cycle. Sunspot activity was very low, solar radiation reaching the earth was therefore light, and the pyramids appeared to be monitoring this course of events.

It wasn't long before people were writing and calling us, stating that for some reason or another their pyramids were not changing milk to yogurt, and failing in other experiments. At this writing, however, sunspot activity is due to increase once again and the pyramids are expected to return to their original effectiveness. Once again our plants will be gyrating from west to east!

Before concluding this chapter mention needs to be made of our experiments with capstones.

One of the great mysteries of the Great Pyramid is the missing capstone. If it existed, what happened to it? Was it composed of a different material than the rest of the pyramid? If so, why? Was it made of a precious material and stolen? We may never know, but one thing seems readily apparent: The capstone, the chambers in the pyramid, and the gabled roof over the King's Chamber work together to enhance the forces within the King's Chamber!

It should be noted that the King's Chamber is not exactly in the center of the Great Pyramid (that is, it is not directly below the apex). While we have referred to the chamber area being in the center, this is roughly the case and we simply let the issue rest. Further experiments, however, particularly with the laser machine, reveal that the offset position of the King's Chamber has other than academic importance.

The room is offset slightly to the south, and the length of the room is not centered beneath the east-west axis but is offset by some feet to the east. Above the King's Chamber are five narrow chambers, and these are topped by a gabled roof, not of granite, but of limestone. It has been generally assumed that the chambers and the gables were constructed to divert the weight of the stones above the King's Chamber. Judging from the construction and the small size of the chambers and gabled roof in comparison to the mass of stone above the King's Chamber, this is not very likely the reason for the design.

Our experiments point to other reasons. A glass pyramid was constructed with indented sides and the top four inches were omitted in order to accommodate capstones of various materials. Two capstones were then made, one of glass and the other of solid plastic. A small replica of the King's Chamber was made, topped with additional small chambers and a gabled roof.

When the hollow glass capstone was installed on the pyramid and the laser beam directed at the west side of the capstone, it was found that the beam of light was directed downward to a point some distance to the west of the King's Chamber.

However, when the beam was directed at the west side of the solid capstone, the ray was first refracted, then directed straight downward and onto the south side of the gabled roof! From there it was reflected to the south side of the pyramid, and again reflected, and entered the King's Chamber on a nearly horizontal plane.

This is important, for the energy flow through the King's Chamber is on an essentially horizontal plane, but the tachyons striking the capstone would be entering the chamber vertically and therefore would be colliding with the horizontal field, which would knock them out of their prescribed paths, thus creating a disturbance and interference waves. But with the gabled roof over the chamber the vertically descending tachyons are reflected from the sloping sides of the roof and are then made to traverse the pyramid in a predominantly horizontal path.

Indented pyramid on mirrored base with laser unit on ball-bearing slide.

These experiments would indicate that the pyramid is, among other things, a universal lens, using only flat planes. We believe that it will be found that the pyramid is, in all actuality, a universal lens, trapping and focusing tachyons, which will be found useful for power and many other benefits to mankind.

In previous writings we have stressed the need for accuracy in the construction of pyramids and our current research emphasizes this need. Throughout we have suggested the use of organic materials in the construction of pyramids. If we are correct in our speculation as to some of the properties of pyramid energy, not only the shape but the composition of the materials used in the pyramids takes on importance.

As we study the nature or organic compounds, the refractive index of various materials, etc., we may find in time the exact materials most effective in regulating the tachyons for specific purposes.

And if we need an incentive to prod us along in our research, we might bear in mind that as awesome as an atomic explosion is, only one percent of the available energy is actually released! But if we can control the tachyon to a workable level, matter could be made to interact with antimatter, thus releasing pure energy.

THREE

The Other Face
of Reality

IF one studies physics, he soon learns that the sand and the rocks and the sea are vibrating atoms and molecules, and that these consist of particles which interact with one another by creating and destroying other particles. One also learns that the air he breathes is bombarded by cosmic rays, particles of high energy undergoing many collisions as they race through the atmosphere. He is told these things through graphs, diagrams, formulas, and mathematical equations.

And, if one is a mystic, he experiences a cascade of energy from outer space, particles pass in and out of being in a cosmic dance of energy. One feels the rhythm and hears the beat of the universe, and he finds himself flowing with the Dance of Shiva.

Probe deeply enough into either and one discovers that physics and intuitive awareness are speaking the same language. Western science has made a habit of going from the particular to the general, of taking things apart in order to discover the nature of the whole. Mysticism, on the other hand, traditionally examines the general in order to decipher the particular, that in understanding the whole or unity of things one can comprehend the pieces.

Which is the best path to truth? Who can say; or what does it matter so long as one arrives? But it is interesting to note that the world's greatest scientists were those who learned to trust other than the rational levels of their minds.

Albert Einstein noted that "Imagination is more important than knowledge."

And Albert von Szent-Gyorgyi proposed that "The basic texture of research consists of dreams into which the threads of reasoning, measurement, and calculation are woven."

When we turn to the writings of the world's greatest mystics, we are amazed how much their observations in the realm of physics parallel those of pioneering physicists. One of these foremost physicists, Dr. Fritjof Capra, writing in *The Tao of Physics,* states: "...The concept of matter in subatomic physics, for example, is totally different from the traditional idea of a material substance in classical physics. The same is true for concepts like space, time, or cause and effect. These concepts, however, are fundamental to our outlook on the world around us and with their radical transformation our whole world view has begun to change.

"These changes, brought about by modern physics, have been widely discussed by physicists and by philosophers over the past decades, but very seldom has it been realized that they all seem to lead in the same direction, towards a view of the world which is very similar to the views held in Eastern mysticism. The concepts of modern physics often show surprising parallels to the ideas expressed in the religious philosophies of the Far East. Although these parallels have not, as yet, been discussed extensively, they have been noticed by some of the great physicists of our century when they come in contact with Far Eastern culture during their lecture tours to India, China and Japan..."

Julius Robert Oppenheimer once noted: "The general notions about human understanding...which are illustrated by discoveries in atomic physics are not in the nature of things wholly unfamiliar, wholly unheard of, or new. Even in our own culture they have a history, and in

Buddhist and Hindu thought a more considerable and central place. What we shall find is an exemplification, an encouragement, and a refinement of old wisdom."

Later in the book mentioned above, Capra states: "...We shall see how the two foundations of twentieth-century physics—quantum theory and relativity theory—both force us to see the work very much in the way a Hindu, Buddhist or Taoist sees it, and how this similarity strengthens when we look at the recent attempts to combine these two theories in order to describe the phenomena of the submicroscopic world: the properties and interactions of the subatomic particles of which all matter is made. Here the parallels between modern physics and Eastern mysticism are most striking, and we shall often encounter statements where it is almost impossible to say whether they have been made by physicists or by Eastern mystics."

Any investigation of pyramid phenomena quickly places the explorer in a position of amazement as to the knowledge and technological sophistication of the ancient builders. Finding they had a highly advanced understanding of the building blocks of life, the modern investigator—living in the age of space and computers—is bewildered as to the source of this ancient wisdom. He may advance the theory—along with Erich Von Daniken—that this knowledge came from highly intelligent and advanced visitors from outer space who managed an evolutionary jump on us by a few thousand years. He may choose to believe that this body of knowledge was evolved on this planet, possibly by advanced civilizations, but has been lost in the dust of time. Or he may find it more comfortable to combine the latter belief with the proposal that there is a mystical channel of knowledge which is able to tap a universal source of wisdom.

Whatever one's choices may be, there is more than a little evidence of an ancient wisdom shared in common by advanced civilizations in the Middle East and Far East hundreds, perhaps thousands, of years ago and protected for centuries from distortion, power struggles, economics, and politics by what became known as the Mystery Schools. There are some good reasons to believe that the marvelous structures of antiquity, in particular the Great Pyramid, were accomplished by persons embracing this knowledge.

This has a bearing on our pursuit of the nature and application of the energy forces produced by pyramid structures for a couple of reasons. One, the possibility of gaining this knowledge in the same manner as did the ancients. Apparently, this information came by way of inner scanning, meditation, and such disciplines of contemplation represented today through the schools of Zen, Yoga, Taoism, Sufism, and Christian mysticism. Secondly, and the issue with which we are here concerned, can we learn anything about energy fields, etc. from a body of knowledge other than Western science? If the ancient Egyptians did not attack the problems of nature with the scientific method, as we understand it, can we learn something from their approach? Apparently we can and even a number of our best scientific minds have vouched for that. Einstein, for example, confessed that he did not figure out the special theory of relativity but that it came to him as in a dream. And Werner Heisenberg stated in *Physics and Philosophy:* "The great scientific contribution in theoretical physics that has come from Japan since the last war may be an indication of a certain relationship between philosophical ideas in the tradition of the Far East and the philosophical substance of quantum theory."

Capra, quoted above, further stated: "If physics leads us today to a world view which is essentially mystical, it returns, in a way, to its beginning, 2,500 years ago. It is interesting to follow the evolution of Western science along its spiral path, starting from the mystical philosophies of the early Greeks, rising and unfolding in an impressive development of intellectual thought that increasingly turned away from its mystical origins to develop a world view which is in sharp contrast to that of the Far East. In its most recent stages, Western science is finally overcoming this view and coming back to those of the early Greek and the Eastern philosophies. This time, however, it is not only based on intuition, but also on experiments of great precision and sophistication, and on a rigorous and consistent mathematical formalism."

We trace our roots of physics to the sixth century B.C. in Greece, where philosophy, religion, and science were not separated. The seers of the Milesian school were little concerned with such distinctions and their goal was to discover the essential nature of things, which they called "physis." We get our word "physics" from this Greek word and it meant, originally, the endeavor of seeing the essential nature of all things.

The Milesians of Ionia had a strong mystical ingredient in their observations. They saw all matter as being alive. As a matter of fact, they did not even have a word for matter, for they saw all forms of existence as manifestations of the "physis," endowed with life and spirituality.

The holistic view of the Milesians was very close to that of ancient Chinese and Indian philosophy. The parallels are even stronger, Capra contends, in the philosophy of Heraclitus of Ephesus. He proposed a world of perpetual change, of eternal becoming. Static Being was to him a deception and he taught that all changes in the world arise from the dynamic and cyclic interplay of opposites and he viewed any pair of opposites as a unity. Heraclitus referred to this unity, containing and transcending all opposing forces, as the Logos.

It is especially interesting to note that Heraclitus credited most of his knowledge as having been learned in Egypt. This was also true of Pythagoras, the Greek mathematical genius. We have given Pythagoras credit for many mathematical equations and as being the father of geometry. Yet Pythagoras made it quite clear that he had gained his wisdom in the schools of Egypt and India. Now the investigations into the mathematical formulas involved in the Great Pyramid would seem to confirm the idea that geometry was much older than Pythagoras.

Once again the question becomes relevant, "What did the ancients know?" They apparently knew something about the forces permeating nature, the commonalities, about the energies we pant after. In seeking an answer to this question on the leeward side of Western science, it is difficult to turn to Egypt today. It is suspected that much of their ancient knowledge is still hidden away, and more than likely a considerable store of wisdom went up in ashes with the burning of the library at Alexandria. Probably our best source of information within the mystical tradition can be found in China and India. What is known of early Egyptian thought closely parallels that of China and India, and in these countries the teachings have changed very little over the centuries.

We cannot, of course, devote many pages to concepts which would require volumes. But we can direct our attention briefly to Indian ideas regarding energy fields, the forces of nature, and levels of reality. The Indian speaks of a universal source of energy as "Prana," and this is referred to in China as "Chi."

A curious thing about Prana or Chi is that as the Far East describes this universal energy it takes on properties which we would describe as electromagnetic, gravity and so on. But in addition there are qualities which we are hard put to find within the domain of positive space-time. Only when we include what we understand to be negative space-time are we able to round out a picture that is as inclusive of phenomena as Prana or Chi. The Indian, however, does not view the world of phenomena so much as one variety being opposed to the other as several levels or expressions of reality existing simultaneously, one transposed on the other. We tend to classify, for example, physical force as belonging to positive space-time and the psychokinetic movement of an object with the mind as falling into the negative space-time category. The Indian, on the other hand, would not consider these two phenomena as being caused by different forces but rather by two expressions of a single force.

The Indian considers all configurations or objects, including his own physical body, as mental constructs. In other words, the world of physical matter is, in any final analysis, not real. It takes on an aspect of reality by that which observes it but close examination reveals the "thing" to not actually exist in that form at all. The "idea" of the "thing" has a certain reality but this is because it is a thought reality. The world of things is an illusion, according to Indian philosophy, and is known as "maya." Maya is what one sees as real until he gains greater wisdom, perceives physical substance as it actually exists; then he understands that it is Prana moving in and out of forms. The forms have a reality only as assigned by the observer.

This model of life is not so different than that of the modern physicist. He tells us that the table, the tree, or our own physical bodies are not static but dynamic. Close examination reveals them to be swirling masses of particles, never at rest, constantly changing. These particles, in turn, are found to be a collection of subparticles, and so on, until all one can really talk about is energy fields. The form, the "thing," in itself has been lost somewhere along the way. And the Indian would say, "Yes, and the energy fields, too, become so subtle, so fragile, that they become lost in thought." What is real is pure consciousness.

Reality plays no role outside of that being, or center of awareness, which experiences the reality. So in the Far East they do not think in terms of various levels of existence. There is only one existence with many expressions. Their separation of non-relatedness has only to do with the ignorance or wisdom of the observer. There are not levels of existence but only degrees of understanding. Sri Aurobindo, the great twentieth-century Indian sage, expressed this well when he explained that it really matters very little whether one thinks of the universe as being physical with spirit being its most rarefied form, or whether one considers the universe as spirit with matter being its most densified form.

In *Raja Yoga* Vivekananda explained the nature of a single reality in stating: "...out of this prana is evolved everything that we call energy, everything that we call force. It is prana that is manifesting as gravitation, as magnetism. It is prana that is manifesting as the actions of the body, as the nerve currents, as thought-force. From thought down to physical force, everything is but the manifestation of prana. The sum total of all forces in the universe, mental or physical, when resolved back to their original state, is called prana...The vital force in every being is prana. Thought is the finest and highest manifestation of this prana..."

It would not serve our turn to expound at length on the nature of reality. But it is of some interest to our subject to reflect that the ancient teachings of the Middle and Far East saw life as a state of perpetual becoming. The ceaseless flow of life through various forms was believed to occur through seven observable levels. An examination of these seven states may help us to better understand the nature of energy. In trying to determine what kind of energy occurs in pyramid space we struggle with electricity, light, magnetism, sound, gravity, and so on. On the preceding pages we have discussed some phenomena as clearly falling into positive space-time and have speculated that some other phenomena may be more at home in negative space-time. Switching to the Eastern model we find the life forces existing along a continuum ranging from dense physical to spirit. All creation starts with spirit and works its way down to the physical. Although all levels interact, each level can be experienced as a separate force. The highest level—spirit—is its own cause and, therefore, is not the effect of something else.

Spirit is, however, the first cause of everything which follows. The seven dimensions of life are: dense physical matter, etheric substance, emotional substance, instinctive mind or substance, intellectual mind, spiritual mind, and spirit. Thus spiritual mind is the effect of spirit but the cause of the five other levels; intellectual mind is the effect of spiritual mind and the cause of the four lower states, and so on until we reach physical matter, which is the effect of etheric substance but does not serve as a cause of anything. It is for this reason that we find the Indian explaining that physical matter cannot be the independent cause of anything. That which is physical has become materialized as a result of non-physical causes.

The dense physical and etheric substance levels would seem to fall into what we have referred to as the tardyon world, the realm of positive space-time. Here we have our bodies, tissue, cells, molecules, atoms, and electricity, light, magnetism, etc., all occurring at or below the speed of light.

The next plateau, emotional substance, would likely fall into the plane of negative space-time. It cannot be measured by instruments except indirectly as it acts upon the levels below. This dimension sometimes is referred to as the astral plane. Things happen on the astral plane instantaneously. The energy initiated by an emotional response can be experienced by a sensitive human receiver at the same moment though thousands of miles away. Those who allegedly have experienced astral travel speak of observing other places and other times— far reaches of outer space or centuries backward or forward in time—in an instant. Up to this point, everything is experienced within a space-time framework. We think of "where" something is or "where" it occurs, and "when" something is, was, or will be. After we pass through these dimensions, however, we are beyond space and time.

The mind and spirit levels do not function in space or

time. An emotion such as love has no dimensions, and a mental picture of a star billions of miles distant requires no time at all. We can jump mentally from a friend's house in Los Angeles to another friend's house in Sydney, Australia, in an instant...and, if we are sufficiently sensitive, we can even accurately observe what our friends are doing at the time. "It is possible," Bob Toben tells us in *Space, Time and Beyond,* "to jump as a single point of consciousness and still have the experience."

This model of life is no longer the exclusive domain of the mystic. "The discoveries of modern physics necessitated profound changes of concepts like space, time, matter, object, cause and effect, etc., and since these concepts are so basic to our way of experiencing the world it is not surprising that the physicists who were forced to change them felt something of a shock," Capra points out, and adds that "Out of these changes emerged a new and radically different world view, still in the process of formation by current scientific research."

In the chapter "The New Physics" Capra further explains: "In modern physics, the universe is thus experienced as a dynamic inseparable whole which always includes the observer in an essential way. In this experience, the traditional concepts of space and time, of isolated objects, and of cause and effect lose their meaning. Such an experience, however, is very similar to that of the Eastern mystics. The similarity becomes apparent in quantum and relativity theory, and becomes stronger in the quantum-relativistic models of subatomic physics where both these theories combine to produce the most striking parallels to Eastern mysticism."

Back to our original point that the mystic has comprehended the universe in a way that now makes sense within the discoveries and theories of the new physics, we can feel greater comfort in the mystical scheme for energy fields. While mysticism in general and Eastern mysticism in particular see the underlying substratum of the universe as consciousness and that in any infinite sense there is no space or time, nevertheless a bridge is constructed from the world as a thought to the world experienced as matter. If the builders of the Great Pyramid were in agreement with this ancient scheme of things, it affords us some idea where they were coming from with their creations. More than this, we may not only understand them better but we may learn something about the nature of energy.

According to Eastern philosophy, the universal energy—Prana—in its behavior is closely akin to electricity, with which it has many characteristics in common, including positive and negative reactions. But Prana apparently goes beyond this expression and serves as the link between the physical and the non-physical worlds. Although Eastern thought conceives of substance as ranging from dense physical all the way up the scale to spirit, only the two lower levels—dense physical and etheric substance or vital energy (sometimes referred to simply as electrical)—exist within space and time frameworks. The higher levels are beyond space and time. The Indian description of the dense physical corresponds with the Western view of positive space-time in which the particles constructing the physical universe move at or below the speed of light. Western science refers to this as the "tardyon" world. On the other hand, the Indian description of etheric substance corresponds closely with Western speculation of particles which move faster than the speed of light—the negative space-time of the tachyon.

The etheric envelope surrounds and permeates the physical body but is composed of substance less dense than the physical. It is the state of physical matter just beyond the gas, liquid, and solid states. The etheric envelope is the exact double or counterpart of the dense physical body and cannot be detected by the five senses, although allegedly it can be seen by psychic sensitives. The observation of the etheric double has prompted the concepts of ghosts and apparitions.

An individual trained to see the etheric double also learns very quickly to see an aura radiating beyond the etheric double, and most clairvoyants contend that there are several dimensions of the aura, ranging from that which is the closest to being physical to that dimension which has properties akin to the next higher level of energy.

A classical text on the aura is A. E. Powell's *The Etheric Double,* first published in 1925. Powell describes four grades of etheric matter: 1) Etheric—the medium of ordinary current electricity and of sound; 2) Super-Etheric—the medium of light; 3) Sub-Atomic—the medium of the finer forms of electricity; and 4) Atomic—the medium for the transmission of thought from brain to brain.

The etheric double has two main functions according to Powell. "Firstly, it absorbs Prana, or Vitality, and distributes this to the whole physical body...Secondly, it acts as an intermediary or bridge between the dense physical body and the astral body, transmitting the consciousness of physical sense contacts through the etheric brain to the astral body, and also transmitting consciousness from the astral and higher levels down into the physical brain and nervous system."

We have readily experienced the non-physical realms of negative space-time through our emotions and thoughts but as these are generally expressed within the framework of space and time we habitually think of them as belonging there. Recent experiments in paranormal activities, particularly telepathy and psychokinetics, have made us aware that we are not limited to our bodies, that our minds are not restricted to our brains, and we are finding ourselves less locked into a space-time framework. Through the agency of the mind there is no real barrier between positive and negative space-time.

We are proposing that the pyramid can slow down the tachyon particle sufficiently that it can interact with particles in positive space-time without losing some of the qualities which make this faster-than-light particle able to provide unusual forces of energy. That these unusual fields of energy can serve as its carrier waves for what is generally seen as psychic phenomena will be further explored.

Dr. Tiller has proposed a non-electromagnetic substance which can serve as the bridge through which energy fields from the negative space-time level can interact with the positive space-time level. He named this substance the "deltron" potential. He proposes that there is a chemical potential of a molecule at the negative space-time level, and that this potential contains a number of field contributions, "one of which is thought to be directly influenced by the Mind level of the universe and a deltron potential term which will be directly influenced by the positive space-time level. In this fashion, coupling relationships exist between all the different levels of the universe, so that everything is interconnected. An impulse at any level creates a set of waves rippling at all levels of the universe."

The interconnection of everything in the universe, that everything is one, has been the philosophy of India and China as far back as history records. As Tantric Buddhist Lama Anagarika Govinda explains: "The Buddhist does not believe in an independent or separately existing external world, into whose dynamic forces he could insert himself. The external world and his inner world are for him only two sides of the same fabric, in which the threads of all forces and of all events, of all forms of consciousness and of their objects, are woven into an inseparable net of endless, mutually conditional relations."

The basic oneness of the universe is not only the central theme of the mystical experience, but it is also one of the most important findings of modern physics. This becomes apparent at the atomic level and it becomes more evident as we probe deeper into matter, into the realm of subatomic particles. Thus we find physicist David Bohn stating: "One is led to a new notion of unbroken wholeness which denies the classical idea of analyzability of the world into separately and independently existing parts... We have reversed the usual classical notion that the independent 'elementary parts' of the world are the fundamental reality, and that the various systems are merely particular contingent forms and arrangements of these parts. Rather, we say that inseparable quantum interconnectedness of the whole universe is the fundamental reality, and that relatively independently behaving parts are merely particular and contingent forms within this whole."

On the other hand mystic Ashvaghosha states, as quoted by T. R. V. Murti in *The Central Philosophy of Buddhism:* "Space exists only in relation to our particularising consciousness."

The same argument applies to time, according to modern physicist Capra. "The Eastern mystics link the notions of both space and time to particular states of consciousness," he states. "Being able to go beyond the ordinary states through meditation, they have realized that the conventional notions of space and time are not the ultimate truth. The refined notions of space and time resulting from their mystical experiences appear to be in many ways similar to the notions of modern physics, as exemplified by the theory of relativity."

Space and time do not exist in any ultimate sense... they are not territories but states of mind? Where does one go with particles? Buddha did away with particles 2,500 years ago. Impressed with the transitoriness of objects, the ceaseless transformation of things, Buddha formulated a philosophy of change and reduced substances, persons, everything to forces, movements, sequences, and processes. He adopted a dynamic conception of reality.

If a particle is not a thing, is it a point in consciousness? What, then, do we do with tachyons, those speedy little flicks of existence whizzing through our pyramids?

Perhaps the question is not whether they exist, but what is the nature of their existence. Matter and antimatter can relate to one another through the agency of the mind, we have said. The more we examine tachyons the more they appear similar to consciousness. Through the power of thought one can move a physical object, levitate an object, communicate instantly whatever the distance, go forward or backward in time, penetrate any barrier. These are also the properties we have assigned to tachyons. Is a tachyon a thought? Whose thought? Is this the substance out of which the Universal Mind wove a universe? Let's reverse the sequence. Are thoughts really things? Do they have substance? What kind of energy are they? Do thoughts travel on a carrier wave of tachyons?

FOUR

The Alchemy of
Pyramid Healing

"**I** WAS recently admitted to the hospital with blood pressure of 260/120 and was informed that I would more than likely be on drugs for the rest of my life.

"Shortly thereafter I read your book, *The Psychic Power of Pyramids,* and constructed an eight-foot-tall pyramid of wood frame and plywood. Each morning before I went to work I spent an hour inside the pyramid, and most every evening I spent two to three hours inside my pyramid. Part of the time was spent meditating and the remainder was spent in reading.

"Within two months, my colour changed from a yellowish sallow back to a healthy colour. And, believe it or not, I am no longer taking drugs and I feel fine.

"My doctor is pleased but at a loss to explain the change. Needless to say, family members and friends are now taking turns with my pyramid."

The above letter was received from Mr. Rodney J. T. Sumpter of Sydney, Australia. We have received many similar letters from people all over the world since the publication of our two books on pyramids. The phenomenon of healing as a result to exposure to pyramid energy or the therapeutic use of water charged in the pyramid was described in *The Secret Power of Pyramids* and discussed more extensively in *The Psychic Power of Pyramids*. Persons have written or called to report on the treatment of a variety of afflictions. The following letter is from Albert Courtney of Tucson, Arizona:

"I have both of your books, *The Secret Power of Pyramids* and *The Psychic Power of Pyramids.* Both of them are very informative and contain many ways the pyramid can be used. I thank you for all this information and the results of experiments by others."

Mr. Courtney went on to explain in his letter that he had a skin problem which was greatly alleviated by the use of water treated inside a pyramid.

We have not encouraged people to use pyramids in the treatment of their ailments as we believe it would be wrong for us to do so. We are not medical doctors and cannot prescribe treatment. We would encourage those with medical problems to see their doctors. But we have had some personal experiences with healing as it seemingly relates to pyramids, and many people have voluntarily and unsolicited reported to us on their experiences. What we have endeavored to do in our writing is to pass along these reports to the reader. We are not trained to evaluate these results.

We have continued to speculate on the nature of pyramid energy and healing, learning what we can from our own experiments as well as others'. There is a great deal of literature, ancient and contemporary, on energy fields and healing. Our search has plunged us deep into medical tomes and into innumerable discussions with medical scientists. But our odyssey didn't end there. It couldn't end there. The picture of man is rapidly changing. Science is stripping the shackles from man and he is emerging as a being much vaster than the vehicle which seemingly contains him. He is (or can be) much more in control, far more creative, and less structured by time and space than we imagined even a few short years ago.

This mushrooming knowledge of man's expanded being places any descriptions of man and his universe far beyond the reach of any single discipline or expertise. What man is has become a question as appropriately directed to the physicist, engineer, and mathematician as to the physician, psychologist, philosopher, and theologian. We turned to them all, along with the medicine men, swamis, and psychics. As we plunge deeper into the unknowns and discover the boundaries of man remaining still beyond, we have learned that the credentials of the mystic are as much and perhaps more in order than those of scientists who do not understand what is occurring all about them and continue to peer into test tubes unaware that the blithe spirit of man has escaped them. So we have gathered our clues and insights where we can find them. Where parallels exist between areas of research, we have endeavored to draw the connections. What may be learned in a medical school laboratory about electrical stimulation of the muscles, for example, may well provide insights applicable to pyramid experiences. On the other hand, what we may learn about changes occurring as a result of exposure to pyramid space may contribute to studies about sensory deprivation, or magnetism and plant growth rates, or whatever.

We have been equally grateful for the letter from the housewife who may confess she knows little about the effects of shape on energy fields but is quite sure that her broken toe healed faster because she treated it in a cardboard pyramid as we are for the suggestions of the trained physicist. We have received both. One man, Jack Mosier of Columbus, Ohio, has done a great many pyramid experiments and his inquisitive mind is quick to pick up on any hints or clues which might be of use to us. He makes notes and sends them along to us, along with any articles which he believes might be of value. For example, Jack found that pyramid-treated water when frozen melted in twenty-two percent less time than an equal amount of the same tap water which was not treated in the pyramid. He speculates this is due to the higher oxygen content in the treated water. Such reports on big or small experiments are a great help because they provide the pieces of the pyramid puzzle.

This type of help is particularly welcome when it comes to the healing process as it appears to occur as a result of exposure to pyramid space. Reports are especially welcome when they come from medical practitioners because they are informed as to the healing process. Their willingness to report is encouraging, for it represents an openness on the part of the scientific community. We were pleased to receive the following note and permission to print from Daisy C. Cotten, M.D.:

"After a visit to the dentist where I had been told that I must have a jaw tooth capped I called Ed Pettit to see if I could come for a visit and a chance to sit in his 'pyramid.' To have a tooth capped is not the pleasantest of experiences so there was a bit of inner anxiety on my part. While at the Pettits' home we spent about forty-five minutes to an hour visiting about their work with pyramid research and enjoyed a leisurely cup of coffee made with pyramid-treated water, then I spent about thirty minutes in the pyramid relaxing. In eight days I returned to the dentist ready to accept the capping. I was prepared for such and given nitrous inhalation for light anesthesia. During the procedure I was aware that the dentist was not preparing the tooth for the capping I had anticipated and seemed to be filling the cavity instead. When it was over my dentist said it was not as bad as he had thought previously, so a filling could take care of it. Many questions go through my mind as to what took place to bring this about. Did an actual change take place in the chemical constituents of my blood which resulted in beginning healing of the tooth? I know how big the cavity in the tooth was originally, and certainly I of my own self could not heal the tooth or make the cavity smaller. Pyramid therapy?

"I was so excited about not having to have the capping that the first thing that popped into my mind I said to the dentist: 'The Father does indeed go before me to make straight my way.' And my dentist said: 'He surely does!'"

Pyramid therapy? Something strange happens inside

of pyramids. In our search to find the reasons why healing apparently occurs, we explored many avenues. Dr. Cotten's experience is reminiscent of our earliest experiments with healing. Actually, the initial discovery was by chance in a way. Mrs. Pettit had been using a pyramid for relaxation and meditation. When she came down with what she believed was a bad abscessed tooth on a weekend and couldn't get medical assistance, she went to the pyramid hoping that she might be able to relax and relieve the pain somewhat. Not only was the pain relieved, but it disappeared and when she visited the dentist on Monday he could find nothing wrong with the tooth. That was several years ago and the tooth is still intact.

This story was related in *The Secret Power of Pyramids,* as was the story of a friend, Judy Fuller, whose dentist was amazed that her gums healed so quickly following an extraction. She spent time in a pyramid immediately following dental surgery. We had some additional experiences with cuts and bruises healing faster after exposure to pyramid space. Meanwhile we were beginning to receive many visits, letters, and phone calls from persons claiming to be relieved of migraines, backaches, ulcers, and a host of other problems as a result of pyramid exposure or the use of water treated in pyramids. They wanted to know what was happening. We couldn't tell them. They were advised to seek medical advice.

From our years spent in the mental health field, we were aware of the fact that the mind can make one ill and it can also make one well. We wondered if we weren't involved in a psychosomatic healing syndrome. Perhaps these people wanted to be well or wanted healing to take place at a faster clip, and it did, thanks to the workings of the unconscious mind. The pyramid was incidental, serving only as a prop or structure for self-healing.

Something new always happens with pyramids, however, and this was to be the case here. Before we could write all of the healing experiences off as psychosomatic, a new phenomenon occurred which would not allow us to so easily dispose of the healing affair. We suddenly started receiving a rush of correspondence from pet owners. These people were allowing their animals to use their pyramids in which to sleep and in some cases they were building cat and dog houses, bird cages, etc., in the pyramid shape. They were reporting that dogs were getting over their rheumatism, worms, were playing as they hadn't played for years; cats were eating better, birds were no longer losing their feathers, and so on and on. We decided that we weren't dealing with only a psychosomatic model of healing after all.

We needed hard data, some objective evidence of changes in the body which we could attribute directly to the pyramid. We got it in the form of blood tests. With the help of a medical doctor and two of his research assistants, we ran skin temperature measurements, took

Sixteen-foot and ten-foot indented pyramids at Pettit's home.

electrophotographs, and ran blood tests on several subjects before and after they spent some time inside of a sixteen-foot pyramid with indented sides. So many variables come into play with electrophotographs of fingertips that we found it difficult—although there were noticeable changes—to attribute the differences to pyramid exposure. The same problem existed with skin temperature readings, but the differences in the blood tests were mind-boggling. As reported in *The Psychic Power of Pyramids,* we discovered that where blood counts—white and red blood count, hemoglobin, blood serum, etc.—were out of normal range before the subject spent time inside of the pyramid, after exposure the measurement was within or had moved toward normal range. If the reading was already within normal range, after pyramid exposure it was more centralized within the range. Sometimes the alteration was drastic.

It should be explained that these tests were conducted on only a few subjects and the results should not be considered by any means exhaustive. These tests have been repeated on a few subjects with similar results, but, of course, in order to be of medical significance the tests would need be run on many subjects. It should also be kept in mind that there is always the possibility of laboratory error. Nevertheless, we feel these measurements are sufficiently important to stimulate further investigation.

Why would these changes occur as a result of subjects being exposed to pyramid space? Again, we are not sure, but the search goes on. Further on in this chapter we will explore the possible relationship of tachyons—the particles which move faster than the speed of light—to the healing process. Meanwhile, however, we might bear in mind that healing of the body and mind may not be a singular or simple phenomenon.

If the human being is only a mechanical-chemical entity produced and maintained by mechanical and chemical forces, then illness and healing are also of this nature. Clearly, a great body of knowledge, experiments, demonstrations, and so on, have revealed man to be considerably more than a bag of chemistry. He is an electromagnetic transmitter and receiver, influencing and influenced by fields near and distant from him. While we speak of his electrical dimensions, these attributes may include electricity and magnetism as we understand them but also other forces we know little about. He has a mind which a growing amount of evidence indicates is separate from his brain and which may not be bounded by either space or time. The philosopher, theologian, and mystic speak of man's soul and whether this is defined as higher levels of the mind or of a higher nature still they can make a pretty good case for its existence.

To understand the nature of healing, then, we may find ourselves looking at it as occurring—or seeming to occur—at several levels. Following our earlier model of the seven levels of man, the problem, and its cure, may originate in the physical substance of the body, in the etheric (electrical) envelope, at the astral level, at the mind level, and so on up the line.

We are familiar with healing procedures which are applied at the mechanical-chemical level, i.e., surgery, drugs, nutrition, manipulation, etc. Pyramid forces do not appear to be directly involved in these applications.

Above this level is the etheric envelope. As this pertains to man's electrical nature, various approaches may be applicable. Thinking in terms of the body as an energy field is not new. Magnetism was used in ancient times to treat various diseases. In A.D. 200 the Greek physician Galen described the magnet as a purgative. The Arabian physician Avicenna used magnets to treat diseases of the liver about A.D. 1000. During the tenth century, in the *Perfect Book of the Art of Medicine,* the famous Persian Physician wrote that magnetism would cure gout and spasms. Swiss physician and alchemist Paracelsus used magnets in the early 1500s to treat dropsy, jaundice, and hernia. American physician Elisha Perkins patented

Perkin's metallic tractors to treat illness and pain in 1776, and it is said that George Washington used them. A short time later Gaylord Wilshire patented his Ionico, a magnetic collar that was promoted as magnetizing blood and curing many ailments.

There have been many serious and some not so serious studies of the various energy fields of plants, crystals, animals, the earth, the atmosphere, and man over the ages. The studies of Mesmer in the latter part of the eighteenth century on "animal magnetism" and his theory of "universal fluid" anticipated some areas of contemporary investigation of bioelectrical fields. Karl Von Reichenbach, a famous German chemist who discovered paraffin and creosote, conducted thousands of experiments on the energy field effects of crystals, plants, and animals. He published his experiments around 1850 and used the term "od" for the energy which he conceived was responsible for the lumination and magnetic effects that he had observed.

Galvani observed a force which he at first referred to as "animal electricity." He decided, however, that he was dealing with an organic energy which differed in many ways from ordinary current electricity. He had many disputes over this with Volta. Eventually Volta appeared to win, yet the records show many fascinating experiments by Galvani and his associate Aldini which are not easily explained in terms of traditional electrical concepts.

Dr. John Kilner, a London physician, conducted studies during the first two decades of this century on the human aura. He used dicyanin (glass treated with a particular dye) screens to make visible the energy field which appeared to radiate from the body. His descriptions of this field—its appearance, how it reflected the physical health and the emotional and mental state of the subject—closely parallel statements concerning the aura by clairvoyants. Current research with electrophotography reports much the same phenomena from pictures taken of the fingertips as well as other parts of the body.

In 1925 L. Gurwitsch used the term "mitogenetic rays" for a radiation he detected emanating from cells. Ten years later two Harvard professors, H. S. Burr, a physician, and F. S. C. Northrup, a philosopher, published evidence in the *Proceedings of the National Academy of Science* for what they referred to as an "electro-dynamic" field in primitive organisms, trees, and animals.

The continuing role of magnetism as a medical tool is evident by scanning some of the patents granted in the last hundred years. At the close of the nineteenth century a variety of articles such as a magnetic hatband, magnetic corset, couch and medallion received patents. As late as 1967 a patent was granted for an instrument which produced controllable magnetic fields for medical purposes. According to the patent application, the instrument was based on previously done work in the field and it also cites work claiming that magnetic fields were able to retard the aging process.

In a paper, "Medical Applications of Magnetism—A New Look at an Archaic Tool," Dr. E. H. Frei, head of the Department of Electronics at the Weizmann Institute, explains that our knowledge of "the direct action of the magnetic field itself is very limited and little is known about the physical and biological processes which may respond to its influence..." He points out that changes may come about as a result of chemical processes being shifted in a magnetic field. "Any process involving movement of ions could be influenced because the path of an ion will change in a magnetic field, and this might be an important factor as ions pass through biological membranes," he states. "There are indications that the action of enzymes is modified in a field. No rigorous theories exist to explain these magnetic effects although rough analyses show that they should be very small in fields up to several thousand gauss [a measurement of magnetism]. However, one can assume that in biological systems even very small effects could accumulate and cause significant changes."

M. M. Labes suggested in a 1966 issue of *Nature* magazine that magnetic fields can influence life processes through liquid crystals. These are intermediate phases between the solid and liquid states which occur in many organic compounds. Sixty years ago T. Svedberg demonstrated that in such oriented liquid crystal systems there can be a marked change in diffusion and in rates of chemical reactions in magnetic fields. Liquid crystals and materials that are near to liquid crystals exist in living bodies, and through these materials the rate of life processes could be influenced.

While there have been contradictions as to results, Frei explains that experiments "have been conducted over a wide range, including tissue cultures, one-celled organisms, plants and animals, and data has been collected from humans. Influences were reported on changes in development and effects on organs..."

Some interesting parallels are found between the healing effects of magnetic fields and those effected by some healers. The results, length of time involved in the healing process, and, interestingly enough, the sensations reported by subjects are in many instances very similar. The comparison is borne out by recent experiments with well-known healer Oskar Estebany. Dr. Justa Smith, an enzymologist at Rosary Hill College in Buffalo, New York, has demonstrated that magnetic fields will affect the activity of enzymes. Learning of Dr. Bernard Grad's work with Estebany at McGill University in Montreal in which the healer affected the germination rate of barley seeds, Dr. Smith invited him to work with her in some experiments. A number of tests were run over a period of time and Estebany clearly demonstrated that he was able to affect the activity of enzymes. His effect was the same as that produced by the magnetic field.

This and other similar experiments would indicate that the force delivered by a healer to an object or subject is of a magnetic nature. This isn't to say that the force is only and exclusively magnetic, but it apparently has magnetic qualities.

When we look at our experiments with pyramids and the many reports on healing we have received, a number of parallels can be drawn between these results and those of applied magnetic fields and those where healers have been involved. Take, for example, the following letter we received from a railroad employee in Topeka, Kansas:

"I read your books on pyramids and was particularly fascinated by the chapters on healing. I decided to build a six-foot-tall wooden pyramid in my basement. I have trouble with arthritis in my hands and wanted to see if the pyramid could help me out. I started out by spending twenty minutes inside the pyramid. I just relaxed during that time while I sat on top of two pillows. By the fourth day I increased my time to forty minutes, one reason being that it just felt good to sit there and just completely relax which seemed a lot easier to do there than anywhere else. Anyway, by the fifth day I started feeling a kind of contracting and then expanding sensation in my hands and feet. The only thing I can liken it to is that it felt like my hands and feet were being pulled in and out by powerful magnets.

"I have continued to use the pyramid now for several weeks and I am amazed ... my hands haven't felt this free of pain and haven't been this mobile for years..."

Assuming that there was an unusual force acting on his hands while he was inside the pyramid, merely the sensation of magnetism does not, of course, confirm that it was magnetic in nature. It well may have been, but other explanations are possible. However, it should be remembered in passing that we found seeds could be germinated faster inside pyramids than without and that plants would also grow at a faster clip. These same phenomena have been produced by both the application of magnetic fields and by healers such as Oskar Estebany, Olga Worrall, and others.

One other parallel may be drawn between the use of magnetic fields and healing and our experiments with pyramids. Russian scientists M. A. Ukolava and Y. B. Kvakina found that agglutination times of erythrocytes and blood coagulation times were affected to some extent by magnetic fields. It has also been shown that blood corpuscles align themselves in the direction of the magnetic field. These findings are noted in light of our experiments with blood changes resulting from subjects being exposed to pyramid space. This is only an observation, however, and additional information is required before anything more definitive can be gleaned from this information.

A magnetic field does not occur in isolation. It produces a current of electricity, as does an electrical current produce a magnetic field. Electromagnetics is playing a larger and larger role in medicine today. This new field of medicine is known as bioelectrical (body electricity) medicine and though still in its infancy it has already launched the instruments and technology to provide us with the means of detecting disease before symptoms are discovered in the body itself. Work initiated by Burr and Northrup at Harvard, mentioned earlier, and expanded since then by others involves the use of a sensitive voltmeter to scan the body. Differences in electrical potential have been shown to represent the presence of disease in the body. Electrophotography—or Kirlian photography—has been used in a similar fashion. Although this technique, which uses electricity rather than light to expose the film, remains controversial, as experimenters cannot agree to what extent the body's electrical field is being photographed or to what degree the exposure is due to outside electrical input, nevertheless most investigators agree that the photographs do reflect changes in physical states. Several reporters, such as Dr. John Lester and Jim Edwards, both of Wichita, Kansas, have demonstrated that electrophotography can be used to select those who do and do not have cancer.

This study was reported in the September 1975 issue of *The Journal of the Kansas Medical Society*. These approaches tend to support the theory that life's patterns occur at the electrical level prior to their manifestation in the physical.

Dr. Raymond Damadian, a medical research scientist at Brooklyn's Downstate Medical Center, spent years researching and another year to build a huge magnet with a bore large enough to hold a man. A medical doctor with degrees in math and physics, Damadian wants to prove that a physicist's tool—nuclear magnetic resonance (NMR)—can detect and possibly treat cancer.

A recent article in *Popular Science Monthly* quoted Damadian as saying that "With NMR, the body's own natural elements can be made to give off radio signals. Then each atom becomes a tiny atomic radio transmitter, broadcasting its situation to the world, and telling what's going on in the chemical world deep inside the tissues."

A student of Burr, Dr. Leonard Ravitz, demonstrated voltage measurements can be used to diagnose the condition of the mind as well as the body. Using a voltmeter, Ravitz measured the depth of hypnotic trances and voltage shifts when the hypnotic states were terminated. His equipment was designed to monitor pure field phenomena such as voltage gradients, independent of resistance and current flow, and without disturbing the body under observation.

Considerable work is under way in Europe, Russia, and this country in determining the effects of electromagnetic and electrostatic fields on the human system. Brain wave experiments reveal that electrostatic fields influence the electrical impulses of the nerves. Other tests have demonstrated that mental alertness improves under the influence of a positive electrostatic field. According to medical engineer James Beal, a positive electrostatic field simulates the reduction of the viscosity index of blood and lymph fluid and this results in the lessening of fatigue and accelerates growth.

It has been found that cell renewal occurs through an ion exchange. An ion is an atom or group of atoms with either a positive or negative charge from having lost or gained one or more electrons. Some waste products of the body are expelled through the skin. An electrical field attracts the surplus or waste ions away from the body surface and this allows for the unhampered renewal of cells. This beneficial effect on the body is apparently the result of the combined action of the positive field and the suspended negatively charged ions in the air. The electric field is the force of motion and the ions are the carriers of the electrical charge.

It has been discovered that we are likely to be surrounded with more positive ions than negative ions. Negative ion generators have been used to improve performance, speed healing, relieve pain, allergic disorders, and depression. Dr. Alfred Krueger, a bacteriologist at the University of California at Berkeley, has been researching negative and positive ions for a quarter of a century. According to a UPI article, he keeps negative ion generators going at both his home and office. He demonstrated that doses of positive ions make mice more susceptible to disease.

Not only have negative ions been shown to affect healing, reduction of disease and improve disposition but persons exposed to a negative ion field report feeling more tranquil, rested and sensations such as in the presence of unusually fresh air. These conditions and sensations have likewise resulted from sitting, sleeping, etc. inside pyramids. It may be that some of the phenomena produced by pyramids can be attributed to an increase in the negative ion field.

Exciting work with electrical fields in the healing of broken bones has been done by Dr. Robert Becker, a medical investigator for the Veterans Administration Hospital in Syracuse, New York. He used a weak direct current and was particularly effective with bones which were not knitting satisfactorily. In one experiment, Dr.

Becker applied low-intensity direct current stimulation to thirteen patients with histories of non-unions in bone healing and realized a seventy-seven percent success rate.

One of the latest reports on the use of electricity in the healing of bones came out in the December 14, 1977, issue of the *Medical Tribune*. It told where Dr. C. Andrew Bassett, an orthopedic surgeon at Columbia-Presbyterian Medical Center in New York, achieved ninety percent healing of thirty children with congenital pseudoarthrosis of the tibia (where nerve defects prevent healing of the tibial breaks). Also, Dr. Bassett and a team of surgeons applied the same techniques to seventy adults with similar healing problems and achieved complete union of the bones in eighty-five percent of the cases.

The *Medical Tribune* quoted Dr. Bassett as saying, "We're learning to talk the electrical language of the cell. By choosing the proper pulse width and frequency distribution for the electromagnetic waveform we can communicate some very subtle bits of information to the cell." Later in the article he is quoted: "It is entirely possible that, in the future, many other functional disorders of the human body can be rectified by changing the electrical environment of cells and organs with specific external messages communicated through an electromagnetic field that is very specific in its pulse characteristics."

In our files are dozens of letters from people who have reported that their broken bones healed in something less than normal time and the only thing they did differently was spend some time inside of pyramids. One of us, Ed Pettit, had a very bad accident with a portable power saw. The fingers of one hand were so severely mangled that the attending physician was not sure he could save the final joints of two fingers. He was certain that the joint of one finger would have to be amputated. As related in *The Psychic Power of Pyramids,* Pettit spent most of his time inside a pyramid during this crisis and when outside the large pyramid, he kept his injured hand in a small portable pyramid. When all of the fingers strangely healed and amputation was not necessary, the physician was so amazed by the healing experience he made the medical file, X-rays, and a personal letter available to us for the above-mentioned book. Feeling has been virtually restored to all of his affected fingers. This is not the history of nerve damage, particularly where the nerves are practically destroyed. The doctor told him that he would not regain feeling but this medical prophecy did not come true.

Electrical currents similar in characteristics to those used by Becker and Bassett involved in pyramid healing? Again, the evidence would point in that direction but there are also reasons to believe that the forces within pyramids are not limited to the electromagnetic spectrum. Could it be possible that universal forces are involved in pyramid healing, running the gamut from physical-chemical, electrical-magnetic, and on through tachyon power, and the subtler forces of mental and spiritual dimensions? Bassett was quoted as saying, "The cells don't care if the potential they experience is from an electrical source or is piezoelectric in origin—they respond with activity in either case." It is believed that piezoelectricity is generated in the King's Chamber of the Great Pyramid from the pressure from the stone above being exerted on the granite walls of the chamber. Does this mean the builders of the Great Pyramid so constructed the King's Chamber in order that it could serve as a healing place? Perhaps. That may be one reason, but we can't find our way back to their intentions. These have been lost in the dust of time, unless some hidden cache of information is unveiled some day. Continued research, however, should provide us with some insights as to the nature of pyramid energy and its applications. If we find answers to our many questions, we can say this knowledge was previously known to the ancients. If this remains conjecture, it fits no more snugly into this category than the reverse position, and it is a little difficult to imagine that such a complex achievement as the Great Pyramid was done with minute knowledge and vacant of intentions.

Electrical stimulation for a variety of medical purposes is claiming the attention of a growing number of medical experimenters. In a syndicated feature for Universal Science News, Inc., David Crossley described a young salesman who was depressed, had back pains, was unable to sleep, and frustrated by the daily anxieties of life. Doctors placed electrodes under his eyes, behind his ears, and a mild electric current was sent through his brain for a half hour to an hour each day. After the third day, his back pains decreased, and at the end of nine treatments his pains were gone, he was sleeping, and he was no longer depressed.

Once again to draw a parallel between the above treatment and pyramid experiences, what we have found repeated over and over again with persons spending time in pyramids are these phenomena. Reportedly, pains have been alleviated, they are able to sleep better and are more rested on less sleep, and depressions dissolve. One young man of our acquaintance had become so depressed and frustrated with life that he couldn't study and had dropped out of his university classes. He was familiar with pyramid research and wondered if it could be of help to him. After spending some time in one of our pyramids, he decided to build his own. His apartment was small but he constructed a pyramid as large as his living quarters could contain. Practically all of his activities were then conducted from inside the pyramid—sleeping, reading, meditating, listening to records, etc. Whether it was the pyramid or some unknown factor in his life, one can't say for sure, but it would be impossible to convince the young man that it was something other than the pyramid, for his life did a turnabout. Two months later he told us that he never felt better or more enthusiastic about life. He had returned to the university and was making good grades.

Pyramid healing: Electricity? Magnetism? Other divisions of the electromagnetic spectrum? Something more?

In *New Light on Therapeutic Energies* Mark Gallert wrote: "Superimposed on what might be called the chemical epoch we can see at least the start of an energy one. It is becoming apparent, from research in various fields, some of which are outlined in this book, that the characteristics of living organisms embrace more types of energy than had previously been realised and include some energy types that have not entered into the field of non-organic science."

Gallert's book contains some interesting summaries of the work of many independent researchers, including Dr. L. W. Eeman, who conducted thousands of experiments on methods of conducting life energy influences from one person to another and who made every effort with control experiments to exclude the presence of subjective factors.

In 1970 many scientists from a number of fields attended the International Symposium on Electromagnetic Compatability at Anaheim, California, and subscribed to the view that: "Probably the farthest off horizon is the possible existence of a new force in nature which penetrates everything; does not attenuate according to known formulas; cannot be measured by conventional electronic test equipment and may have a spectrum of its own. It has many names, such as a second force of gravity (gravitons), eloptics, hydronics, dowsing, radionics and radiesthesia, to name a few. Modern electronics is beginning to stumble over them but has no means of tying into them for practical answers."

There are energies emitted by living organisms, particularly the human being, which seem to defy the laws of nature as presently understood. As discussed earlier, experiments in mental telepathy, mental projection, precognition, psychokinesis, etc. demonstrate that whatever energy is involved in these phenomena cannot be blocked by Faraday cages or shields designed to serve as a barrier to electromagnetic fields. Further, these forces seem to function outside of space and time.

Earlier in this century Dr. Wilhelm Reich conducted experiments through which he proposed that there existed a primordial cosmic energy. This energy, which he referred to as "orgone," permeated, he said, all living things. He explained that whereas electromagnetic radiation was the product of the breakdown and transformation of mass, in accordance with quantum physics, orgone energy, on the other hand, was pre-atomic, mass-free energy from which under certain conditions mass particles could form.

One doesn't have to entirely agree with Reich in order to appreciate his work. It is encouraging that a growing number of scientists are losing their timidity sufficiently to take another look at his experiments. Today they are finding it impossible to discuss bioenergy without reference to Reich's studies.

Reich's theories implied the existence of a universal substratum to existence. This concept is in line with the East Indian idea of "Prana" as the universal energy, with the various forces of nature being expressions of this singular underlying force. Baron Karl von Reichenbach had contended that though the mysterious oric force might resemble animal magnetism and was associated with it, it also could exist quite independently. Years later, Reich held that—as quoted by Peter Tompkins and Christopher Bird in *The Secret Life of Plants*—"the energy with which the ancient Greeks and the moderns since Gilbert were dealing was a basically different energy from that with which the physicists are dealing since Volta and Faraday, one obtained by the movement of wires in magnetic fields; different not only with regard to the principle of its production, but fundamentally different."

Tompkins and Bird further state: "Reich maintained that matter is created from orgone energy, that under appropriate conditions matter arises from mass-free orgone, and that these conditions are neither rare nor unusual. All of this further suggests that in living matter there exists, below the level of Lavoisier's classical molecular chemistry, a deeper level of nuclear chemistry which associates and dissociates nucleons, the components of atomic nuclei."

Paris chemist Professor Louis Kervran presented some highly controversial concepts in 1972 with the publication of his book *Biological Transmutations.* He clearly demonstrated that the mechanisms for the transmutation of biochemical elements exist within man. For example, if you need iron, you can take organic manganese and your body will convert the element into iron.

"The serious error of scientists consists in their saying that reactions occurring in living matter are solely chemical reactions, that chemistry can and must explain life," Kervran states in his Introduction. "That is why in science we find such terms as 'biochemistry.' It is certain that a great number of manifestations of life are produced by chemical reactions. But the belief that there is only chemical reaction and that every observation must be explained in terms of a chemical reaction is false. One of the purposes of this book is to show that matter has a property heretofore unseen, a property which is neither chemistry nor nuclear physics in its present state. In other words, the laws of chemistry are not on trial here. The error of numerous chemists and biochemists lies in their desire to apply the laws of chemistry at any cost, with unverified assertions, in a field where chemistry is not always applicable. In the final phase the result might be 'chemistry,' but only as a consequence of the unperceived phenomenon of transmutation."

Kervran's work is important, for the principles of biological transmutation affect every phase of our existence. What we hear Kervran saying is underlying all substances are pre-chemical states. Chemically there does not seem to be a connection between iron and organic manganese and yet organic manganese is transformed (transmuted, actually) within the body into iron. The bridge, apparently, does not occur at the chemical level but at a pre-chemical level. This would be in keeping with the electrodynamic principles of life which propose that all physical substances and forms have a prior existence in the etheric or electrical state. Kervran's principles would also agree with Eastern and mystical views that physical substances, and their chemical constituents, are the final stage of a series of occurrences, with the stage just previous to the physical being the etheric. Kervran is saying that the "switch" takes place when organic manganese and iron, for example, are reduced or transmuted to a state where they share common properties. This same principle applies when the "magnetic energy" of the healer is transmuted into healthier blood cells or organs of the patient. On the surface, there does not appear to be a bridge between the thought energy I am generating from the pressure of my job and the very physical ulcer in my stomach, but we can understand the interaction when we stop identifying thought and ulcer as two separate existences and look behind them to their common properties.

Kervran has stated that "The kind of energies to which the great Austrian scientist and clairvoyant Rudolf Steiner refers as cosmic etheric forces must exist, if only from the fact that certain plants will only germinate in springtime no matter what amounts of heat and water are administered to them during other parts of the year..."

"We do not know what matter really is," Tompkins and Bird quote Kervran. "We do not know what a proton or an electron is made of, and the words serve only to cloak our ignorance. He suggests that inside atomic nuclei may lie forces and energies of a totally unexpected nature and that a physical theory to explain the low-energy transmutations with which he deals must be sought, not in the hypotheses of classical nuclear physics based on powerful interactions, but in the field of hyperweak interactions in which there is no assurance of the operation of the established laws of conservation of energy or even the existence of a mass/energy equivalent."

The alchemists of the medieval ages were ridiculed or ignored by most scientists. But in light of today's scientific findings, the alchemists may have suspected certain principles in nature but simply did not have sufficient knowledge and technology to provide concrete evidence for their ideas. Kervran's transmutation is not a change in the periphery of atoms, as we would expect in the usual chemical reactions, but in the nucleus of the atom. This is possible according to nuclear physics, but those approaches require an energy expenditure millions of times greater than what we have believed takes place in living organisms. Nuclear chemists transmute elements in large accelerators where small, charged particles are brought to very high energies in order to smash the atoms. The concept that a flower can transmute silicon into calcium must be difficult for a nuclear physicist to handle, especially since calcium has an atomic number which is higher than silicon.

The principles of biological transmutation throw a different light on the phenomenon of materialization and dematerialization. More on this in a later chapter. What is of interest to us here is the possible explanation of some aspects of pyramid phenomena. With pyramids we are apparently dealing with low-energy transmutations rather than forces such as nuclear physics uses to smash the atom. This, as Kervran suggests, is the type of transmutation we find throughout nature.

In the tests we ran taking blood samples of subjects before and after they sat in a large pyramid, it was found that the blood serums had changed. With one of us, Schul, the iron was .46 parts per million before entering the pyramid. The normal range of iron is 1.20 parts per million. Following the session in the pyramid, Schul's iron count had changed to .98, actually doubling and moving much closer to normal range. Another subject, Brenda Scott, had a zinc count of .80 prior to entering the pyramid and a zinc count of 1.12 parts per million after pyramid exposure. The normal count for zinc is 1.00 parts per million. Where did the iron and zinc come from? This phenomenon would appear to be a case of biological transmutation resulting from the low-energy stimulation of the pyramid.

We, and several other experimenters, have run experiments with water, the results of which are interesting to explore within the context of biological transmutation.

Our experiments, described in *The Psychic Power of Pyramids,* were run with ordinary tap water. Samples were taken to a laboratory and the bacterial count determined. The samples were then divided into experimental and control groups, with the containers being identical. The experimental samples were placed inside pyramids and remained there for about two weeks. The controls were either placed simply outside the pyramids or, on other occasions, placed inside of containers being of the same material and of a volume equal to the pyramids'. After two weeks, experimental and control samples were taken to the laboratory for testing, and it was found that the bacterial count in the pyramid-treated water was significantly less whereas the bacterial count in the control samples had increased considerably.

Equipped with these findings, we decided to test water samples for mineral content. The tests were conducted in the same fashion and it was discovered that the mineral content in the pyramid-treated water was significantly less while the mineral content of the control water remained essentially the same. Again, we would appear to be dealing with biological transmutation.

Indian and Chinese philosophy point to energies which incorporate the known forces of nature but also energy not limited to these forces. Included would be pre-atomic, mass-free energy from which mass particles can form. The Far East—which gave birth to acupuncture—talks about the importance of balancing the energies of the body. Disease is caused by imbalance. In China and

Japan the force is twofold and is known as "Yin" and "Yang." Acupuncture is a method of channeling, short-circuiting, and manipulating the flow of Yin and Yang in such a fashion as to bring balance to the body. While we usually think of this twofold flow as positive and negative, in the sense of polarity principles as used in electricity and magnetism, there may be another dimension that is not yet fully explored. As Oriental philosophy is woven around the concept of a universal source of energy in which everything is contained, the positive-negative principle may also imply both positive and negative space-time. The balance of the physical body might imply, on one hand, positive and negative electrical fields; it might be kept in mind that psychic functions appear to fit better in the negative space-time of the tachyon.

In any case, the universal energy appears to work for the balance of its parts, which, according to this model, would include the human body. The tachyon may be the agent of balance and may function partly through the process of transmutation. In other words, it moves materials about until they are correctly balanced. If the pyramid proves to be the bridge between positive and negative space-time it would be the ideal tool of alchemy.

If we could allow that the tachyon is nature's balancing force we can begin to understand why the forces within the pyramid appear to be selective. The question we have often been asked is "Why does the energy within the pyramid always seem to work for the benefit of man?" How often we have asked ourselves this question, for we have been constantly amazed by this phenomenon, as, for example, when an edible plant will thrive and a poisonous one will die inside the pyramid. But if the correct pattern occurs at the electrical level and becomes deteriorated and destroyed by abuse, disease, contamination, pollution, etc., then nature may work through electrical and higher energy forces to bring the form back to its original pattern. This is not a fanciful idea, for the human body has amazing recuperating powers; a cut finger heals and a bruise disappears; and water will eventually purify itself if left alone. Although our subjects were not exposed to pyramid space for a great length of time when we ran our blood tests, nevertheless the various properties of the blood were adjusted in the direction of normal range. Some force seemed to be a balancing influence.

Taking another look at our water experiments, this same force appeared to be bringing the water back to a purified state. In the 1920s, Ernest Rutherford obtained hydrogen atoms from such elements as nitrogen, sodium, gold, aluminum, and phosphorus. It is reasonable to speculate that a force capable of permeating all matter, such as the tachyon, could, as it traversed molecules of hydrogen and oxygen, so regulate the liquid water as to transmute the unwanted minerals and change copper, zinc, iron, etc. into hydrogen or the inert gas nitrogen. Laboratory tests of water by some researchers have shown that water treated in the pyramid does increase in nitrogen content. This may be one reason why plants treated with pyramid water do better than those watered with untreated water.

The selective process also seems to prevail as regards the presence of water. Water, of course, is both beneficial and detrimental, depending upon where and to what extent it is applied. Water applied in proper amounts to living things is beneficial, thus we find that plants inside a pyramid make use of a larger quantity of water and grow faster than plants outside. On the other hand, water applied to non-living matter such as iron promotes rust and we find within the pyramid razor blades retain their edge for a longer period of time as the forces acting upon the blade appear to drive out the water dipoles. Non-living matter, such as meats, vegetables, and fruits, are preserved for longer periods when placed inside pyramids as a result of the dehydrating effect of the energy within the pyramid. Controlled tests have also demonstrated that sodium hydroxide pellets absorb less water while inside a pyramid as opposed to control pellets placed within other shapes.

Earlier we cited research indicating a change in the decay of radioisotopes placed in pyramids. In view of this study, one wonders if transmutation might also apply to radioactive materials. Life requires radioactivity as it is needed for the continued burning of the sun. Radioactivity within the human body, however, is a different matter. In his book *Only a Trillion* Isaac Asimov speculates that the damage done by the radioactive decay of carbon-14 in the body is much more likely to be responsible for spontaneous mutations than potassium-40, as some scientists contend. He goes on to say that if this is the case "there is precious little that can be done about it unless someone turns off the cosmic rays, or unless we build underground cities." We can't help wonder, however, how relevant it would be to add "or unless we build pyramid homes, office buildings, etc."

We have previously mentioned the apparent absorption of tachyon energy by aluminum without a measurable increase in heat. If this proves to be the case, then perhaps the tachyon is being used by nature not to heat the body, as the absorption of photons would, but to produce the opposite effect of cooling. This sensation is frequently reported.

The fresh air effect, including the noticeable lack of odors within the pyramid, should also be considered. Ultraviolet light has long been used to purify air. Many effects reported from pyramid studies reveal similarities akin to ultraviolet light. Can the tachyon, in flooding the interior of the pyramid, indicate qualities similar to ultraviolet light? We may find that the velocity of tachyons is sufficiently reduced within the pyramid to have a frequency close to the ultraviolet spectrum. The velocity, however, will largely depend upon the nature of the material used in the pyramid's construction.

Let us imagine a tachyon as it speeds through space.

Being an infinitely small point, it penetrates the nucleus of an atom of hydrogen. It immediately picks up a slight amount of energy from the nucleus and this slows and broadens it somewhat. As it travels on it passes through an atom of iron, let's say. The tachyon gives up some of its energy. It speeds up and its width is narrowed. Finally, let's say, it encounters the energy-rich solar wind flowing to and around the earth. It feeds on this energy, slowing and widening as it does so.

Suddenly our hypothetical tachyon encounters the wooden wall of a pyramid. It gluts itself on the energy of the atom of the material and its girth so expands that it is too large to penetrate the opposite walls of the pyramid. It merely rebounds. Well-fed and bouncing about, it now contacts a living body, and as the tachyon passes through the nuclear envelope of the cells, the nucleus is stimulated to impart the right amount of energy to cause the cells to vibrate at their optimum level. We do not know, of course, that this happens, but there is strong evidence that the force with which we are dealing does behave in the manner that scientists are now assigning to the theoretical tachyon. Rather than a single tachyon, however, millions of the fleeting particles would be involved.

If our imaginary tachyon, speeding along toward the pyramid on the solar wind as it moves over the earth from a westerly direction, encounters a metal building to the west of the pyramid, it becomes diverted from its appointed task.

Envision the condition of our astronauts in their space lab. What effect, do you suppose, the aluminum walls of the spacecraft had on their bodies? Would the shielding from the tachyon flow have any bearing on the fact that calcium was deficient in their bones when they returned? If this was the reason for the deficiency, then why were not the plastics and inner lining of the craft effective in making the tachyons more tractable? Could it be that the miles of wiring cramming the interior of the craft caused the benefits of the inner lining materials to be ineffective? In any case similar conditions render a pyramid ineffectual.

If it does turn out that the aluminum skin of the craft is responsible for the occupants receiving less than the required amount of tachyons, what would be the result if the craft was composed of metals which had been exposed to the interior of a pyramid-shaped storage shed for some time prior to assembly of the craft? As we reported previously, aluminum tends to block the energy forces from the interior until the aluminum becomes saturated with the energy and it then no longer serves as a blocking agent. Aluminum foil placed inside of a pyramid tends to absorb the available energy, restricting its accessibility to anything else, until the foil becomes saturated. Once this occurs, the foil can be used outside of the pyramid as a substitute for the pyramid as it imparts this energy to other objects. For example, meat wrapped in treated foil has been kept for quite some time without refrigeration.

Long airline flights commonly cause "jet lag" in passengers and crew. They feel down in the dumps for no apparent reason, although this condition is usually ascribed to changes in sleeping and eating cycles. Is this the case, or is it the result of close confinement inside the shell of unenergized aluminum?

As we speculate on the nature and properties of an energy force which appears to be beyond the already known forces of nature, we are not alone. Not only are some of the world's leading physicists, physicians, and parapsychologists trying to grasp the elusive force, but a famous biologist, Austrian Paul Kammerer, stated the following in *Allgemeine Biologie:*

"If transgressing the frontiers of what is permissible, I should finally state what seems to me to be the most probable—an unproven and at the present time, unprovable scientific credo—then I have to say: the existence of a specific life force seems to me highly plausible! An energy which is not heat, nor electricity, magnetism, kinetic energy (including oscillation and radiation), nor chemical energy, and is not an amalgam of any or all of them but an energy belonging specifically to only those natural processes that we call 'life.' That does not imply that its presence is limited to these natural bodies that we call 'living beings' but that it is present also at least in the formative process of crystals. A better name for it, to prevent misunderstanding, might be 'formative energy' instead of 'life energy.' It possesses no supraphysical properties, even though it has nothing in common with physical energies already known. It is not a mysterious 'entelechy' (Aristotle, Driesch), but a genuine, natural 'energy'; however, just as electrical energy is connected to electrical phenomena, so this 'formative energy' is linked to living phenomena and the development and change of forms. Above all, it is subject to the law of the conservation of energy and is fully capable of conversion into other forms of energy..."

The Indian Upanishads had a way of putting it:

> *It moves. It moves not.*
> *It is far, and it is near.*
> *It is within all this,*
> *And it is outside of all this.*

FIVE

Psychic Powers and the Fifth Force

A NUMBER of psychics of our acquaintance are able to perform unusual card tricks, but recently we have worked with a young lady with something more than the usual paranormal talents. Without touching the deck, she can tell you what cards you hold in your hand. But the uniqueness of her skills rests in her ability to control your choices. You are not aware that she is doing this; you do not feel her presence inside of your skull, yet she is there telling you to select this card over that card. It is an amazing feat and it is extremely difficult to block her manipulation.

Because of her unusual abilities, we have been working with this person in efforts to learn more about her powers. Our tests included having her sit inside of a pyramid and we found that her skills were even greater under this arrangement than before. Before we could carry out any statistical studies on this experiment, however, other demands were made on the young woman's time. The reason for mentioning our work with her is because of an unusual experience. A laboratory assistant had spent the day with her and they had been working with some biofeedback equipment. The experiment consisted of the young woman demonstrating control over not only her own blood flow but that of others. I (Schul) had brought along a new experimental pyramid. She sat inside the pyramid for several minutes and stated that she felt an intense energy field all around her. She suggested that I try it to see if I felt the same field. While still seated inside of the pyramid, she picked up a deck of cards and stated that she would run through them while telepathically telling me what they were.

After several complete misses, I started getting distinct images of certain numbers and shapes in the center of my forehead. A number of near misses followed and then I hit a number of cards correctly. Several years before when working steadily with cards I had been able to raise my score well above the chance mark. But I had not been practicing and even when practicing regularly I had not been able to come close to my accomplishments that day sitting inside a pyramid with the young woman acting as sender.

I did not fare too well either inside or outside of a pyramid when someone other than the young woman was handling the cards. But it is interesting to note that my scores with her were better when I was inside the pyramid. Again, time did not allow for us to establish significant statistics on this exercise, but it illustrates what people are beginning to discover about themselves and pyramid space.

It is known that some people are more psychic than others. The reasons for this are not adequately known. Except for their unusual paranormal skills, most psychics are not different than average individuals. Apparently they have access to other dimensions of themselves not experienced by most persons but there is growing evidence that psychic abilities can be improved with effort. Researchers, such as Charles Honorton at the Maimonides Medical Center in Brooklyn, have shown that psychic skills correspond to states of deep relaxation and the production of alpha brain waves. Alpha states occur as the subject withdraws his attention from external distractions and instead focuses on internal states of awareness. This inner scanning and withdrawal from the world outside oneself tend to shift the awareness in the direction of the intuitive mind. The differences between the psychic and the non-psychic have not been found by means of examining the organic brain. The differences apparently exist at the level of the non-physical mind rather than the physical brain.

As explained earlier, the mind apparently functions in the realm of tardyons moving at or below the speed of light and tachyons moving faster than the speed of light. The mind is as comfortable in negative space-time as it is in positive space-time. Psychic abilities can be justly described as perceptions or sensitivity which extends beyond normal perception and sensitivity. A person functioning at the latter level will see himself as subject and that observed as object. Psychic awareness, however, tends to move subject and object closer together until, within the awareness of the true mystic, space and time provide no barriers and the world seemingly outside himself is more clearly understood, for he experiences the world as part of himself.

But this is no longer just the language of the mystics. Atomic physics has arrived at the position of explaining that particles or universes have no meaning outside of that which observes them. As physicist Fritjof Capra explains in *The Tao of Physics:* "Quantum theory has thus demolished the classical concepts of solid objects and of strictly deterministic laws of nature. At the subatomic level, the solid material objects of classical physics dissolve into wave-like patterns of probabilities, and these patterns, ultimately, do not represent probabilities of things, but rather probabilities of interconnections. A careful analysis of the process of observation in atomic physics has shown that the subatomic particles have no meaning as isolated entities, but can only be understood as interconnections between the preparation of an experiment and the subsequent measurement. Quantum theory thus reveals a basic oneness of the universe. It shows that we cannot decompose the world into independently existing smallest units. As we penetrate into matter, nature does not show us any isolated 'basic building blocks,' but rather appears as a complicated web of relations between the various parts of the whole. These relations always include the observer in an essential way. The human observer constitutes the final link in the chain of observational processes, and the properties of any atomic object can only be understood in terms of the objects' interaction with the observer..."

So close have the findings of atomic physics become to those discoveries of the mystic that one has to check references to be certain of the source. For example we find Sri Aurobindo stating in *The Synthesis of Yoga:* "The material object becomes...something different from what we now see, not a separate object on the background or in the environment of the rest of nature but an indivisible part and even in a subtle way an expression of the unity of all that we see."

In order to be able to perceive the reality of nature, not as separate units of matter, but as interacting and interconnected fields, the mind must be capable of perception at all levels of reality. Such observations apparently must take place both below and above the speed of light. In the worldwide best seller *Jonathan Livingston Seagull,* Jonathan discovers that the true secret of life resides at the speed at which one moves. He learns to fly extremely fast and in doing so learns many things beyond the understanding of the other seagulls. One day Jonathan dies but on the other side he finds he can fly even faster than before. Regardless of his speed, however, he is never quite satisfied because it is still limited. Admiring his unrelenting zeal, his wise old teacher gives him a cue: "Perfect speed, my son, is being there..."

Perfect speed, of course, is infinite speed and infinite speed means being in all places all of the time. Then there is complete unity, oneness, and non-separation. The spiritual state is beyond space and time, according to the mystical tradition. In the Eastern cosmological system we find seven gradations of substance: physical, etheric, astral, lower mental, higher mental, spiritual soul, and spirit. Only a few years ago this model was ignored by Western scientists as presenting no basis for scientific exploration. But in light of technological breakthroughs which allow us to explore other dimensions of man, to speak in terms of fields rather than configurations, and speculate on particles moving faster than the speed of light, the Eastern model is gaining greater attention from Western scientists whose credentials are quite in order.

Thus we find Stanford University physicist Dr. William A. Tiller using the model of the seven substances in his address, "Future Medical Therapeutics Based upon Controlled Energy Fields," presented at the Ninth Annual Medical Symposium of the A.R.E. Clinic in Phoenix. He suggested that we expand our concepts as to the nature of substance and envision it as having seven distinct levels. Each of the levels has unique dimensions and laws. The energies of the various levels, Tiller suggests, interpenetrate and interact with each other only weakly under normal conditions, for they have different energy bands. They can be brought into strong interaction, however, by means of the mind.

Tiller's model considers the physical or positive space-time frame as having the lowest energy band. The next higher level is called the negative space-time frame and it is the opposite or mirror energy system of the physical. The third level is a transitional level or the bridge between space-time dimensions and non-space-time dimensions. In some literature this is referred to as the astral plane. This energy band appears to be the level on which our emotional natures function. The next three levels are levels of the mind: instinctive mind, intellectual mind, and spiritual mind. The seventh and last level is that of spirit. The last four levels are all non-space, non-time levels of the universe. These cannot be effectively described by means of language inasmuch as our physical perceptions must operate in space and time.

"Therefore," Tiller states, "this model consists of two important groupings of energy levels. The first is a space-time construct that we may think of as an enlarged physical frame, and this is embedded or enfolded in a non-space/non-time construct which is interfaced via the transitional frame. Space and time seem to be properties of this embedding frame, just as mass and charge are properties of electromagnetic energy in the space-time frame. Events taking place in the non-space/non-time frame are thought to alter the metric of space-time and thus the corresponding event characteristic of that frame."

According to Tiller, substance functioning in the negative space-time frame consists of magnetic monopoles which are bound together to form atoms and molecules that travel faster than the speed of light. They cannot be observed directly by our five physical senses nor by any instruments yet developed.

We speak of the tachyon's tremendous speed but it becomes apparent that we are still not dealing with anything close to infinite or absolute speed. The tachyon is not Jonathan's "perfect speed," but it is interesting to note that the faster he went, the more he understood. It seems that in order for perceptions to be beyond those of our five senses, the speed must be greater than at the level on which they function. Paranormal powers seem to operate at higher frequencies. These powers evidently function according to different laws and seem to fit within what is known about negative space-time rather than within positive space-time. For example, psychic powers cannot be blocked by an electromagnetic barrier such as a Faraday cage; psychokinesis—the movement of physical objects by alleged mental powers—defies mechanical laws and gravity... actually demonstrating levitation instead of gravity; telepathy takes place instantly and appears to defy space; precognition seems to operate outside of any time consideration, and so on.

As Dr. Tiller has explained, the higher levels of the

mind may operate completely beyond any space-time framework. But as the mystics have long contended, psychic powers are not synonymous with spiritual powers and, therefore, may function not beyond space and time but somewhere between that level and the realm of physical matter. That zone, according to Dr. Tiller and what we described earlier, would seem to be the mirror of physical reality—the world of particles moving faster than the speed of light, or negative space-time.

The reason that psychic powers emerge when a person is exposed to pyramid space, or become more intensified, may be due to the pyramid's action of slowing down tachyon particles and making this energy accessible to man's psychic dimensions. A provocative study of the increased psychic function stimulated by pyramid exposure was completed recently at Central State University in Edmond, Oklahoma.

The experiments were conducted by psychology major Tom Garrett to complete requirements for an Experimental Psychology course instructed by Dr. William A. Fredrickson, psychology department chairman.

Following is Garrett's account of the experiments:

"In the spring of 1977, I was a member of a research team at Central State University. The members of the team consisted of Marc Pate, Vicki Ficklin, Mary Lee Garrell, and myself. It was our desire to test the influence, if any, the pyramid had in regard to human telepathic ability.

"The experiment was designed not to prove the existence of 'pyramid energy' or to prove that sitting under a pyramid model will enhance a person's ESP powers, but rather this was one of the first attempts (to our knowledge) to bring the pyramid into the laboratory under strict scientific experimental controls.

"It was our belief that in order to establish if the pyramid did cause a change in ESP scores, we would naturally have to eliminate as many factors other than the pyramid that could cause a difference in the scores. To begin, all subjects were given prerecorded instructions as to the mechanics of the ESP test. The reason for this was to eliminate any verbal influences that could affect the experimental outcome. This was necessary because it has been shown in the past that the experimenter can set the mood in either a positive or negative light before the test, therefore causing an interference in testing even before the testing begins.

"All subjects were given a standard ESP test using the methods developed by J. B. Rhine of Duke University. The deck of twenty-five ESP cards consisted of five star symbols, five cross symbols, five wavy line symbols, five circles, and five squares.

"The subjects were randomly assigned to control, experimental, and bogus conditions. The telepathic ability of the twelve subjects in the bogus group were tested under a slightly distorted pyramid, accomplished by breaking the base line on one side (to neutralize the energy effect and to test for the placebo effect). The twelve subjects of the control group were tested under similar conditions but with the exclusion of the pyramid structure. The experimental group of twelve persons was tested under a true pyramid. The pyramid employed is referred to as the Modular Pyramid System and was manufactured by Pyramid Products of Glendale, California (a six-foot open-sided aluminum pyramid). Each subject was run through four trials consisting of twenty-five cards each for a total of one hundred responses. Each time the subject 'guessed' the right symbol, it was recorded as a hit.

"The results of the experiment can be explained by the phrase, 'I've got some good news and some bad news.' After all testing was completed, an analysis of variance was run on the university computer using a two-factor mixed design with repeated measures on one factor (individual trial scores for each group were employed for this analysis). The pyramid group compiled a group mean (average) of 5.30; the bogus pyramid group a mean of 4.68, and the control group a mean of 4.29. The pyramid group therefore averaged 1.01 more 'hits' per trial than the control group, but the mean was obviously not beyond the chance level.

"After the means and standard deviations were completed, we noticed what appeared to be a significant difference between the pyramid group and the control group up to the fourth trial. Through three trials of the ESP test, the pyramid group's mean was 5.80 while the control group's mean was only 4.10, a difference of 1.7 'hits' per trial. It was then decided to test for significance again, only this time employing another statistical test (for the 'stat' buffs reading this, it was a 3 by 3 analysis of variance using the two-factor mixed design with repeated measures on one factor).

"The computer now indicated a significant main effect for the pyramid group. To put it simply, we found significance at the $p.01$ level which indicates that the pyramid group was significantly higher than the other two groups $(F[2,33] = 7.66, p.01$, with a required value of $F[2,32] = 5.34)$. It did not, however, indicate a significant main effect for trials or interaction.

"It is apparent that nothing was proved by our experiment, but from a scientific standpoint, this issue certainly deserves further research and replication. It became clear to me that we have now entered into an area of psychological research that requires a full understanding of the true nature of man. When undertaking research in these areas, it cannot be clear as to what extent the experimenter is affecting his experiment. Therefore, the secret power of pyramids may be in the unlocking of man's full mental and spiritual potentials. Once again we pull the cosmic trigger.

"Since the time of our experiment, our team has graduated and moved away from the university. However, we are all continuing our research through an organization called Pyramid Research Associates (PRA). Our focus at this time is understanding ourselves better to understand the meaning of the pyramid more fully. Although we have depended on the laboratory methods in our experiments, it is wise not to ignore subjective feelings when dealing in these areas. I would like to thank Bill and Ed for this forum and would close with this brief quotation from Erich Fromm's *Psychoanalysis and Religion:*

" 'Academic psychology, trying to imitate the natural sciences and laboratory methods of weighing and counting, dealt with everything except the soul. It tried to understand those aspects of man which can be examined in the laboratory and claimed that conscience, value judgments, the knowledge of good and evil are metaphysical concepts outside the problems of psychology; it was more often concerned with insignificant problems of man. Psychology thus became a science lacking the main subject matter, the soul...' "

If the pyramid does increase one's paranormal abilities, what kind of forces are involved?

We received one report of an experiment which indicated that radioisotopes decay at an accelerated rate. While this experiment has not been confirmed, it is interesting to consider the possibilities in light of mind-over-matter experiments using isotopes. Remy Chauvin of Strasbourg University used a Geiger counter to measure the emissions of uranium isotopes while test subjects were attempting to alter the decay rate. The subjects were instructed to "will" an acceleration of the radioactive process for one minute; to slow it the second minute; and the third minute they were to make no attempt to alter the process. This cycle was repeated many times over a fifteen-day period. It was found at the end of that time that the subjects could increase and decrease the radioactive process. Helmut Schmidt of Duke University found that his subjects could achieve similar results with odds of ten million to one against chance.

These tests would tend to support our earlier thesis that

the human mind and the pyramid can serve as the bridge between tardyons and tachyons...that both can slow down the tachyon to the extent that it can interact with the physical world. When the human mind is exposed to the tachyon-enriched environment of the pyramid, it may activate other dimensions of its functioning.

That some other force is involved than electromagnetism in paranormal activity has been demonstrated by a number of scientists. One of the most careful studies was conducted by the famous Russian physicist Leonid Vasiliev. He used a hypnotist to send telepathic messages to his subjects. After it was found that the subjects were responding telepathically to the hypnotist, Vasiliev determined to learn whether the carrier wave was of an electromagnetic nature.

Dr. John Taylor, professor of mathematics at King's College, London, reports on this experiment in his book *Superminds:*

"What was needed was to screen out any possible electromagnetic waves that might be transmitted from the hypnotist to the subject. Two such screens were made, one of ironplate, the second of lead. The latter was essentially a lead capsule with a lead lid which slid along grooves containing mercury. In addition, the subject was placed inside an iron cage which helped to keep out electromagnetic radiation even more effectively. These elaborate shields failed to present any barrier... Distance seemed to have no effect on the strength of the transmission; exactly the same success rate was achieved with a distance of 1,000 miles between hypnotist and subject. These results apparently destroyed the hypothesis that electromagnetic radiation was being used, since the lead and iron shielding were expected to deflect such radiation completely..."

Under the careful arrangements of Harold Puthoff and Russell Targ at Stanford Research Institute, Uri Geller—famous for his metal-bending feats without the use of physical force—sent a Geiger counter into a loud wail by means of mentally willing it to do so. He also bent objects placed in containers shielded from electromagnetic fields.

One should not overlook, while referring to experiments in which electromagnetic forces were blocked, that some experiments with paranormal powers have revealed the presence of strong electrical and magnetic fields. Russia's Dr. G. Sergeyev, for example, found that when Nelya Kulagina was moving physical objects around without touching them the electromagnetic field surrounding her was ten times that of a normal person. The electrical potential at her back was fifty times greater than that at the front, whereas most people only have three or four times as much. Our experiments with pyramids have indicated the presence of an electromagnetic field. However, some of the results—as with Geller and others—cannot be explained by means of electromagnetic fields. There well may be more than one process or field at work in the case of Geller, Kulagina, et al. and all paranormal phenomena. We are not in any manner ruling out electromagnetism as a factor in pyramid results. What we are suggesting is that the pyramid—and the human mind—may serve as an interface mechanism allowing tachyons to interact with electromagnetism and the other known forces of nature.

Physicist Dr. Jack Safritti refers to biogravitational fields as gravitational forces which perform in two different ways within the human system. It would appear that when he speaks of "inside the light cone" he is referring to what we have been calling positive space-time, and that "outside the light cone" refers to negative space-time. In *Space, Time and Beyond* he states: "The biogravitational field, like all gravitational fields, acts in two distinct ways: it can be 'seen' (inside the light cone), but even more important it can be 'felt' (outside the light cone). In the first case, we refer to signal processing in ordinary channels of perception through the known senses. In the second case, we refer to the tachyonic (instantaneous) mode of interaction, which psychic researchers have called the paranormal channel. I conjecture that these two information channels affect one another in data processing by the brain."

Safritti turns to quantum theory to explain forces beyond or in addition to electromagnetic ones. The word "quantum" comes from the word "quantity" and refers to "a certain amount." Quantum theory proposes that the emission or absorption of energy by atoms or molecules is not continuous but occurs in discrete amounts, each amount being called a quantum. Safritti was present during some of the experimental tests of Uri Geller's psychokinetic powers. He proposes that the existence of psychokinetic powers hinges on the ability of consciousness to control the biogravitational field. This in turn interacts with ordinary gravitational fields.

"Specifically, I suspect," Safritti states in *Space, Time and Beyond,* "that the tachyonic action of the gravitational field...can be connected with the quantum potential... The quantum exerts quantum forces that act in addition to the more familiar electromagnetic forces."

In a paper entitled "A Suggested Interpretation of the Quantum Theory in Terms of 'Hidden' Variables," Dr. D. Bohm states: "Thus, the quantum mechanical forces may be said to transmit uncontrollable disturbances instantaneously from one particle to another through the medium of the...field...What does this transmission of forces at an infinite rate mean? Our interpretation can give rise to no inconsistencies with relativity...general relativity indicates that the limitation of speeds to the velocity of light does not necessarily hold universally."

Safritti further states: "The stability and strength of matter depend on the interplay between the quantum and electromagnetic forces. For example, quantum tunneling of a particle through an electromagnetic energy barrier occurs because the quantum force momentarily cancels out the electromagnetic barrier. If consciousness controls the biogravitational field and if there is a significant coupling of biogravitational to ordinary gravitation, then there is a direct contribution of consciousness to the quantum potential."

Quantum force, as it is being used here, apparently refers to a force outside of or beyond that to be found in the electromagnetic spectrum. The field in which psychic phenomena occur has been referred to by various writers as "psychotronic," "psychoplasma," "bioplasma," "psi power," and so on. As psychic phenomena and paranormal powers appear to operate independently of space and time structures, most scientists agree that these forces do not fit within the known forces of nature. Gravity is one of the known forces, but Safritti refers to "biogravitational" fields and these clearly are something different than just gravity as it normally applies to the human body. It would seem that biogravitation is an attribute of or at least can be brought into activity by way of the mind. If the latter, the mind apparently serves as the interface between gravity and biogravity. If gravity is the pull toward the center, biogravity may be the thrust away from the center. If gravity is the force organizing physical matter, biogravity may be the force organizing conscious substance.

Such a model may be more than an arbitrary structure. It is compatible with the Oriental concept of equal and opposite powers. According to the Eastern tradition, as life disintegrates on the spiritual level it moves toward organization on the physical level, and as life disintegrates on the physical level it reorganizes on the spiritual level. The bridge between the world of matter and the world of spirit is the mind. Psychic phenomena occur when the mind—acting as a bridge—allows non-physical forces to interact with the physical world. According to our earlier model of tachyon forces, not only the mind but the pyramid—not only because of its composition but due to its shape—can sufficiently slow down tachyons for them to interact with particles moving at or below the speed of light.

It should, of course, be kept in mind that "tachyon" is a

word, as is "psi," or "psychotronic," etc., and one is no more sacred than another. Their use reflects efforts to define a force which doesn't fit into the attributes of other forces. As this applies to pyramids and psychic phenomena, things occur which cannot be entirely confined within time and space structures. Perhaps space and time are only positions of observation or conditions of consciousness. This is what the mentalist would tell us—that in the final analysis everything is consciousness, that the world begins and ends there. Thus the Hindu refers to the universe as the "Dream of Brahma," and the British scientist Sir James Jeans tells us that the closer he looks the less the universe appears to be a great machine and the more it appears to be a great thought.

The mystic finds no problem in dealing with matter and mind, space and time, they all run together in their flow within a singular existence. And the great Indian sage Sri Aurobindo tells us that it really matters very little whether we consider the universe as physical and spirit as its most rarefied form, or whether we consider the universe as spirit with matter being its most densified form.

Perhaps this is what our minds are trying to tell us and maybe even this is what the ancient builders of the Great Pyramid are echoing through the ages to us.

In any case, pyramids produce some unusual effects, including enhanced psychic powers to those exposed to a pyramid's space. In order to better understand these phenomena we find ourselves in the company of both the mystic and the scientist. The former experiences it and the latter has a way of studying it. Neither can be ignored.

Safritti makes one of those attempts in *Space, Time and Beyond* when he states:

"I believe the gravitational distortion of space and time predicted in Einstein's general theory of relativity provides a possible scientific explanation of precognition, retrocognition, clairvoyance and astral projection, provided we accept the additional postulates that individual consciousness can alter the biogravitational field of a living organism and that the biogravitational field distorts the local subjective space-time of the conscious observer. Thus, a participator in a high state of consciousness can artificially create blackholes and whiteholes in his local biogravitational field..."

Safritti suggests that consciousness can so distort time that its rate of flow to an observer is not the same as it is with the object being observed. Through this difference in time flow the observer may be able to see into the probable future or past of the object being observed. Safritti believes this is the likely biogravitational mechanism for precognition and retrocognition.

Earlier we discussed Tiller's work with the Yoga philosophy of the seven levels of substance: the physical, the etheric (which the Russians call bioplasma and some researchers have referred to as the energy body or pre-physical body), the astral, the three levels of the mind, and spirit. We come back to it here because it serves our turn well. Though an ancient concept, it has sustained the wear of time and is now in the enviable position of being acceptable to both mystics and a growing number of scientists. It helps us to understand all kind of phenomena—ranging from the dense physical to the spiritual—for they are not viewed in an unrelated way but are the individual expressions of a singular force. In order to understand them, however, in a scientific rather than in a mystical fashion the various levels must be seen as producing different configurations while following different laws.

Our present definitions of human energy fields are inadequate to account for paranormal phenomena. So many things happen which cannot be understood in terms of the known forces of nature that we will only become confused if we try to fit them into a mold which cannot contain them. Tiller tells us that it is at the level of the mind that one can bring about changes in the organization of structure in the various levels of substance. He states: "That is, through mind forces, one can create a pattern, and that pattern then acts as a force field which applies to the next level of substance. In turn, that force field is a force organizing the atoms and molecules into configurations at that level of substance. That pattern of substance at the etheric level, then, is in a particular state of organization, and it has its own radiation field—its own force field if you like—and that force field, then, is a field for the organization of matter at the next level of substance—the physical level of substance. These etheric forces, then, bring about the coalescence and organization of matter at the physical level of substance.

"Here, we see something that I have chosen to call the 'ratchet' effect; one can see an action beginning at the mind level and working its way down through to produce an effect on the physical level (and vice versa)."

The most significant thing about a pyramid is its pattern. Our experiments have led us to believe that not only does a physical pattern of the pyramid exist but that this particular unique pattern also exists at the etheric level. In fact, the etheric or energy pyramid exists whether or not there is a corresponding physical one. The etheric pyramid forms the physical one, rather than the other way around. This corresponds to Tiller's "ratchet effect." Following this reasoning it is not difficult to envision that the ancient builders of the Great Pyramid "saw" or "experienced" the pyramid in its exact form before they established its physical construction.

In *The Secret Power of Pyramids* we related the experiences of philosopher Paul Brunton during a lonely vigil one night in the King's Chamber of the Great Pyramid. He was visited by a spirit priest and after some unusual experiences was told that the real secret of the pyramid existed within himself. The significance of the pyramid, apparently, does not reside within its physical substance, nor within the observer's cells and tissues, but at some higher level. The highest form of the pyramid exists at the spirit level; secondly, at various mind levels; then, etheric level; and finally at the physical level. But there is something about its form that "ratchets" down to the physical plane. However, its force field can be intercepted at non-physical levels and apparently at the etheric level this is precisely the correct pattern to produce interactions between physical forces and non-physical forces. This is also the "twilight zone" of psychic phenomena—activities which partake of both physical and non-physical fields.

Reasons have been presented in our previous writings and elsewhere in this book for claiming that enclosed pyramids work better than open or pole pyramids. Our experiments have led us to believe that enclosed pyramids present a better field for the interaction between subluminal, luminal, and superluminal particles. Nevertheless, many claim excellent results with open pyramids. It may even be possible to mentally construct a pyramid and have it work. More than a few have claimed to accomplish this feat. The mystic doesn't have any problem with this. Neither does the psychologist. Every day he witnesses what mental constructs of fear, love, anxiety, hate, etc. can do to physical bodies. If the attributes of a pyramid are partially mental, then a mental pyramid will work. If the qualities of a pyramid are partially etheric, or electrical, then an etheric pyramid will be to that extent successful. If the importance of a pyramid resides in its pattern, then it makes little difference how substantial the materials are which are used to form that pattern. The advantage of an enclosed pyramid may be found in that being enclosed does not distract from any of the above functions but added to these are the reflective and refractive planes which apparently contribute to the activity of both electromagnetic and tachyon forces within the pyramid. If there is such a thing as a perfect pyramid, it would be the one which most correctly corresponds to the etheric pyramid which has fostered it. The most perfect etheric pyramid, in turn, would be the one most like the mental pyramid which created it, and so on.

We are so used to thinking in terms of building something physical and hoping that it produces the desired results on other levels that it is difficult to envision matters occurring in an opposite fashion. But according to the new physics and the models we have been using this is the case.

New research is supporting the earlier contentions of Galvani and Mesmer that all living things have electrical or magnetic properties, yet few have been suggesting that they must have about them the same electromagnetic fields as those accepted in the world of particle physics. This was exactly the thoery advanced by two Yale University professors a number of years ago, but their bold theory has been mostly ignored by the scientific community.

The professors, one a philosopher, F. S. C. Northrup, and the other a medical doctor and neuroanatomist, Harold Saxton Burr, asserted that electrical fields are the organizers of the life system. After many years of research and thousands of experiments in measuring "life-fields" with sensitive voltmeters they considered the fields of life to be the basic blueprints of all life. They discovered that such illnesses as cancer could be diagnosed before the usual symptoms developed; that the healing of wounds both internal and external could be continuously monitored at a distance; that internal processes such as ovulation could be accurately monitored according to changes occurring in the electrodynamic fields of a woman's finger.

Burr measured the voltages of the electrical fields around frogs' eggs, and the area producing the highest-voltage reading always became the frog's nervous system. He found that there was a distinctive pattern of energies that would later form the blob of protoplasm into each element of the physical body.

Burr also worked with plants. He found there were life-fields around seeds, and discovered that profound changes in the voltage patterns were caused by the alteration of a single gene in the parent stock. Of even greater importance was his discovery that it is possible to predict how healthy a future plant will be from the electrical diagnosis of the seed.

Burr's student Dr. Leonard Ravitz found that life-fields also reflect people's mental states. He found that he could monitor altered states of consciousness, changes of emotions, and varying degrees of hypnosis. Burr and Ravitz believed that just as our bodies and brains are maintained by permanent electromagnetic fields which mold the ever-changing material of the cells into a pattern, so in turn these fields are influenced by the greater fields of the universe.

Burr's life work, as further developed by Ravitz and others, indicates that the organizing field around the bodies of living things anticipates the physical events within them and suggests that the mind itself can change the field. Thus, mind or the thought-field becomes the higher agent of change. Again, it apparently serves as the meeting place between the physical world and a refined form of energy or a higher-octave force existing beyond the electromagnetic spectrum. Evidently, the pattern exists as a thought-field prior to its establishment on the electrodynamic level and, consequently, the physical level. This concept supports Tiller's seven levels of substance and his ratchet effect.

"It seems almost beyond human comprehension at the moment," Joseph Goodavage states in *Magic: Science of the Future,* "but there does seem to be some kind of eternal, universal, interflow of countless forms of energy—from the tiniest known fields within the atom to supercolossal gravitational and other fields of the planets and even stars and galaxies—which exert their power over vast cosmic distances. It's conceivable that endless hierarchies of energies, some spanning the entire Universe in a single instant, exist in multidimensional stages. The universal L-field [life-field] may be but a single manifestation of these highly refined forces."

Electromagnetic fields are easily measured but the "highly refined forces," including thought-fields, are not so accessible. This is equally true of the energies involved in psychic phenomena. They occur within the physical domain but their causes appear to be other than physical. One of the scientists who agrees with Tiller's model of positive and negative space-time is physicist Dr. James B. Carlton. In order to understand psychic phenomena he explains that we need a bridge between them and the world of matter. This is what is so exciting about pyramid research—it offers through the medium of a physical object a way to explore several levels of activity. Perhaps the invisible pyramids within ourselves can provide us with all of the answers, as we suggested in *The Psychic Power of Pyramids,* but until we arrive at those higher states of knowledge it is our belief that the extended pyramids in basement, workshop, and laboratory can serve as one of our gurus. As the human mind apparently journeys between the invisible and visible worlds, so may the pyramid subscribe not only a pattern in space but also serve as the reflection of a non-physical design.

In any case, Carlton tackles the problem of translating psychic phenomena in terms of their interaction with physical substance and he joins Tiller in proposing a model of tachyons and negative space-time. In a paper, "Insights into the Role of Body Energies Through Auric Phenomena," presented at the Ninth Annual Medical Symposium of the A.R.E. Clinic in Phoenix, January 1976, Carlton stated that most models as to how psychic phenomena occur have been rejected on the grounds that they do not provide a bridge with the physical world. He explained that the negative space-time idea does provide this bridge or interfacing.

"In accordance with the model," he stated, "it is currently theorized that humans have two sensory systems: 1) one for sensing physical nature or the positive space-time frame and 2) one for sensing any phenomena in the negative space-time frame. These can be appropriately referred to as the positive and negative space-time sensory systems...

"During the occurrence of a psychic event, the negative space-time frame laws appear to override those of the positive space-time frame, ruling the appropriate physical laws null and void only for the interim. Accordingly, these are a 'higher' set of laws that can be altered and/or constructed by the human mind, and this implies that we are not totally bound to the physical world.

"...as one seeks to obtain more information through the use of his negative space-time sensory system, more of his positive space-time sensory system must be given up. Conversely, if more positive space-time sensory system information is sought then the negative space-time sensory system is mentally suppressed. Again, we apparently cannot have both simultaneously to a high degree. Throughout life we find ourselves in natural situations in which we are turning on one sensory system as we turn off the other and vice versa. For example, one practicing the art of meditation seeks to still the physical or positive space-time senses. If he is sufficiently successful, the negative space-time sensory system is activated as a consequence and unusual experiences can occur. If indeed we turn off one as we turn on the other, we might be led to suspect that ultimately in the death process, the negative space-time sensory system is absolutely maximized as the positive space-time sensory system is absolutely minimized..."

If our theory is correct and there is an increase of tachyon activity within pyramid space, then the subject exposed to this space is stimulated by the negative space-time sensory system. He finds it easier to meditate, time and space are distorted, the physical world is less with him, and his paranormal powers are increased. Experiments to date bear this out.

Our studies indicate, as do the theories of Safritti,

Tiller, Burr, Carlton, et al. If we understand them, that tachyons gain access to the human system via the non-physical mind. The mind acts upon the brain; the brain, in turn, acts upon the physical body. This occurs whether or not a person is inside a pyramid. But due to the action of the pyramid slowing down the tachyons so that they can better interact with the human system, the pyramid appears to be a particularly rich field for this occurrence. Meditative states apparently contribute to the activation of the negative space-time sensory system because attention is focused away from the physical world and awareness is less centered in the physical brain and more in the non-physical mind. Again, because of the tachyon action, meditation is particularly profound inside of pyramids, as many people have reported. The girl Kathy C., who will be discussed in the following chapter, started unfolding when she became involved in meditation, and apparently she made even greater gains when she did her meditation inside of a pyramid.

SIX

Help for the Mentally Retarded

A MOST interesting case of a retarded girl who suddenly started changing after years of no real improvement came to our attention. The young woman's mother traveled several hundred miles to visit with us after reading *The Secret Power of Pyramids* and *The Psychic Power of Pyramids*. She came to elicit our suggestions following some unusual experiences with her daughter.

That the girl had been guided into meditation and shortly thereafter had started responding in completely new ways to herself, to others, and to her environment—and that following the use of a pyramid for her meditations her behavior pattern took another meaningful turn—is a story worth telling. It has vast implications not only for the retarded but for all of us.

For a good many years science talked about the human being as a living organism composed of a body, nervous system, and brain. Somehow out of its mechanical-chemical makeup it produced emotions, thoughts, motivations, aspirations. If you couldn't put your finger on it, in some manner locate it in time and space, it wasn't real. It had to have substance, measurable substance, or it just didn't exist. Science almost convinced us of this—despite religion's argument to the contrary—before it was discovered that physical substance itself didn't really exist. This turnabout allowed us to legitimately talk about mind as something separate from the brain. Within this still developing model the brain has been relegated to the position of an instrument under the command of a non-physical mind. This position changes a great many things. Hopefully, it also explains many things which were a mystery when consciousness was a product of the mechanical-chemical workings of the physical brain. Now it is mind which is the creator. Mind creates the brain, or, as some are now saying, consciousness exists apart from and independent of the brain, but consciousness on occasion—as needed—creates what we have come to know as a brain. The mystic applauds and is tempted to say, "I told you so."

Well, this is a different ball game, isn't it? It takes the shackles off the human being and gives him free access to the universe. When he was locked within the confines of physical matter, he was limited to whatever skills, talents, functions, etc. that this bondage allowed. If something physically was damaged or destroyed, then the human being was limited accordingly. When awareness was merely a function of the brain, then damage to the brain meant damage also to the consciousness. Those who were classified as mentally retarded were found to have some brain disfunctioning and so it was believed that they were doomed to a life of limited attentiveness and perception.

The mystic speaks of realms of experience, of knowing, which do not lend themselves directly to functioning on this planet. There are levels of reality, he says, which do not necessarily coincide with material reality. Although he knows, he finds it difficult to express this knowledge in words, pictures, or schemes that others will understand. Our children, however, do not grow up in a mystical world. They are surrounded by people whose awareness is limited for the most part to the brain. They do not understand life as a whole but only in parts as collected by their five senses and as put together by the left hemisphere of the brain. Their ideas are manufactured of things, objects, and their concepts are couched within the framework of space and time. Relationships are understood within a three-dimensional world.

Usher in a human being who may be as aware as anyone else, because his consciousness is intake, but that consciousness finds itself trying to relate to the world of substance with an imperfect instrument. Problems immediately occur. While the mind may be performing perfectly well, the brain isn't computing, so the world of things doesn't come in as clearly, and language is as difficult for this individual to cope with as a mystical experience is for the normal person. Communication and any real relationship between the so-called mentally retarded and normal individuals are extremely difficult. And, of course, the mentally retarded find it difficult to successfully manipulate a physical body or cope with the environment.

Undoubtedly, at some level the mentally retarded or brain-damaged person "knows" but it does not serve his turn so well among those who are materially oriented beings. One is reminded of the boy Pete in the long-selling novel *Shepherd of the Hills*. To his Ozark neighbors he was considered slow-witted, yet in some ways he was more perceptive than others. Although he couldn't express himself, now and then he would say, "Pete knows," and somehow one had the feeling that he really did.

While involved in some medical research several years ago I (Schul) had the opportunity to spend several days at Dr. Evarts Loomis' health clinic—Friendly Hills Fellowship—in the San Jacinto Mountains southeast of Los Angeles. During my stay I became good friends with a teenage mentally retarded boy who was there for treatment. We swam and took walks together and I think we developed a kind of psychic rapport between us. In any case I shall never forget one particular moment that we shared. One afternoon I spotted him sitting quietly alone in a cluster of trees. When I drew near I saw that he was contemplating a large great-horned owl perched on a branch above his head. Then I realized that his eyes and those of the owl were locked in a meditative embrace. Neither he nor the owl gave any indication that they were aware of my presence. I sat down on the grass and waited, moved and somewhat awed. After a time the boy's head turned and he looked at me. It was momentary I am sure but in that instant I felt as though I was looking into the eyes of a very old and very wise man. Those eyes were fathomless and open to the universe. Then he grinned, jumped up, and asked if I would run through the woods with him.

Einstein once noted that man uses less than ten percent of his brain. Faced with that figure, we can't help but wonder why we don't use more of our gray matter, and why, if we don't use all the brain, anyway, the mentally retarded can't simply use other parts of the brain and do as well as most of us. The answer is not that simple, for the brain is many times more complex than any other computer. However, medical science has of late learned a great deal about the two halves of the brain. It has been found that the left hemisphere of the brain is the seat of the rational mind and that the right hemisphere is the seat of the intuitive mind. Until this decade the right hemisphere was largely ignored as it was believed to be a weak duplicate of the dominant left hemisphere. It is now believed to play an equally important role. While the left hemisphere handles linear reasoning, perceptual relationships, language, etc., the right hemisphere apparently is the facilitator of creativity, intuition, and imagery. The left hemisphere sees the world in pieces and tries to fit it together. The right hemisphere perceives the wholeness or oneness of things. But we are used to speaking of life in pieces and bits, so the intuitive mind, although more holistic, does not have a language with which to express itself. The mystic is likely to say that what he has experienced is ineffable or indescribable.

It is exciting to learn that science is now confirming what the mystic has long contended, that there is an intuitive mind. The right hemisphere of the brain is not the intuitive mind but appears to serve as the instrument of the intuitive mind. If the intuitive mind is developed, we are told that our awareness would be enormously expanded. Unfortunately, in our culture this has not been encouraged and the talents of the right hemisphere have been neglected. This is changing, however, as medical scientists, educators, theologians, and philosophers in growing numbers have come to realize the value of the intuitive mind. To develop this portion of our mind is like finding the other half of ourselves, and in order to accomplish this goal many people are turning to meditation, Zen, Yoga, Tai Chi, biofeedback training, and other disciplines designed to open new doors of the mind.

The goal of these growth activities is not to escape into another world but rather to expand untapped resources and to put us in touch with dimensions of ourselves which may have remained hidden. The above-mentioned disciplines, and some others not mentioned, when practiced correctly, will help unfold a more sensitive, alert, controlled, intelligent, and intuitive individual. This person will be more functional, not less, on this planet.

What if a mentally retarded person successfully practiced a growth discipline and started demonstrating new alertness, perceptiveness, learning abilities, and creativity? This would indeed be exciting. It would give us new hope in exploring unrealized potentialities in the handicapped. But, as meaningful as this is, there are other implications involving all of us. If meditation, let's say, accomplishes something for the retarded, then it tends to support our position that the intuitive mind is a reality; that the consciousness of the retarded may not be damaged on the intuitive level; that the mind is not synonymous with the brain; and that channels can be opened whereby the mind can learn to respond on this level. In this case, the mentally retarded person has provided us with confirmation that the mind is quite independent of the brain. Further, this occurrence would also lend support to the mystical concept and conscious- ness model of some scientists that the mind creates the brain. If this is the case, the degree of one's awareness would not be locked into an unchangeable brain. We have been led to believe that intelligence is limited to the state of the brain and that a damaged brain cannot be repaired. Training may occur, other areas may be used, but there is a limit, according to the textbooks with which we are familiar. The new models of consciousness would say otherwise.

Why is it, then, that we have witnessed the limiting factor as regards people's intelligence quotients? In other words, why do they seem to be limited to a certain range of intellectual functioning? Also, why is it that we can train mentally retarded persons to perform better but only within certain limits? If our above model is correct, the answer to these questions would seem to reside with the fact that our efforts have been directed toward the physical brain and, more specifically, the left hemisphere of that physical brain. As explained above, the brain— being physical itself—operates within the material domain of objects, configurations, space-time frame- works. The material world's limitations are the brain's limitations. But Dr. Paul Torrence clearly demonstrated at the University of Minnesota that standard IQ tests do not measure a person's total awareness, perceptiveness, ability to do original thinking, and creativity. In our culture we have played to those who are left-hemisphere- oriented and neglected those who perform best in the right-hemisphere arena. According to our model, our ability to perform left-hemisphere activities depends on how good a computer our mind wishes to build. It is not a static condition. It can be improved. But even though our mind decides not to improve on our brain-computer, there is still the mind quite apart from any instrument it might use. In some cultures this is referred to as the higher mind to distinguish it from the lower or rational mind. German philosopher Immanuel Kant referred to these levels of awareness as "practical reason" and "pure reason."

Within the mystical tradition, the rational mind is limited to inductive and deductive reasoning and subsequent conclusions. However, since the rational mind is limited to reasoning about observations produced by senses which see only an extremely narrow focus of the world, and to experiences only partially understood, its conclusions are forever in error and must be constantly revised. The intuitive mind, however, does not add up and subtract bits of information imperfectly perceived, but is in contact with consciousness itself. Its knowledge is derived directly from the source and it has not gone through the process of compounding errors.

We have played our games with bits and pieces, atoms and molecules, things and objects, space and time. But we ran our feelers into outer space and they still went beyond, and we divided things into the smallest particles and they disappeared into energy. We couldn't locate our world of matter any more. It disappeared while we toyed with it, with all of its causes still intact. The rational mind took us to the threshold of matter but it couldn't help us any more. We were forced beyond the mind of things to the mind of not-things. Instead of training our brain to compute more and more data, our search for truth led us to that state of awareness which didn't deal in matter. Our brains did rather well with particles which moved at or below the speed of light, but how could they cope with something beyond their realm of experience? They helped us with a process of elimination, so we could keep throwing things out of the box and saying, "That isn't it either."

Now it is another ball game. With the causes behind the world of effects residing somewhere else and the secrets of life still in the great beyond, it has dawned on us that we have to go on to the higher mind. The religious and mystical world say that the philosophers' stone is to be found in the realm of the spirit and not in matter. The new physicists are saying the same thing, it would seem, when they point the way to antimatter, beyond the tardyon to the tachyon, a shift from positive space-time to negative space-time.

But how do you get there from here? Aren't we tardyons ourselves? How do we get to the other side without getting lost in the process? Apparently we are both tardyons and tachyons. Part of us clings to the world of matter and part of us soars in the realm of the spirit. The bridge between the two is the mind. The task of the disciplines mentioned earlier is to train us to be dwellers on two planets.

Let us suppose that our mentally retarded subject through meditation was able to bridge the two worlds. In doing so she would experience a breakthrough by taking what she was experiencing at the mystical or intuitive level (and most likely had been experiencing for some time but could not bring it consciously into focus or expression) and be able to apply it to her environment and in her contact with others.

Let us further suppose that our subject combined her meditation with sitting in a pyramid and experienced additional changes. What could this mean? It might mean that she had placed herself in a field that was serving to act as the interface between positive and negative space-time. Part of her mind—the brain—would be stimulated by the tardyon field of electromagnetic forces and thus it would be expanding its potential. Another part of her mind—the non-physical intuitive mind—would be stimulated by the tachyon field of magnetic-electric forces, as Dr. Tiller refers to them. By stilling all outside activity through meditation the two minds could interact. A new awareness and attentiveness could be experienced at the conscious level.

There is evidence to indicate that the mystical experience, out-of-the-body experiences, extrasensory perception, transcendental states, clairvoyance, etc. fall within the domain of negative space-time. Such experiences give the subject the feeling of "being somewhere else," of having "passed through an opening," or "being on the other side." More on this later, including some considerations of why these experiences are easier to come by while exposed to pyramid space, and results of ESP experiments inside of pyramids.

Meanwhile, our "supposing" with a mentally retarded subject will be shifted away from fiction. These were real experiences. They happened to Kathy C. of a Midwestern metropolis. (Her parents have asked that her complete name and address be withheld in order to protect her from the merely curious. The parents, however, would like to be of assistance to any qualified person doing research in this field. Any professional person wishing to contact the parents should send a letter written on official letterhead to either of us in care of the publisher and it will be forwarded to the girl's parents.)

Kathy is twenty-five years old, is a (trainable) moderately retarded person. She has been in structured training programs for the past eighteen years. She seemed to reach her plateau six years ago and very little improvement was seen until she was introduced to meditation. Speech remained her greatest handicap. She spoke only two-syllable words and could not pronounce every syllable. She requires assistance in dressing and her food is cut for her. "While she comprehends everything you say, she never showed any amount of creativity to use this knowledge or participate socially," Kathy's mother stated. "She has had the same diet for five years and there have been no changes in her working or living conditions to effect any of the reported changes."

The mother has kept a careful log on all of Kathy's activities for a number of years. Mr. and Mrs. C. became interested in transcendental meditation four years ago.

"From the moment of our first TM lecture four years ago, I recognized the potential of TM for the retarded; however, it was not until we had been meditating two and a half years that we were fortunate enough to have a teacher of TM living with us and willing to work with Kathy. The results were amazing and have continued ever since," Mrs. C. stated.

She continued, "I would say that the only knowledge Kathy had of TM before she began was that she did recognize that it was a quiet time for us and would shut the door if we were meditating. I have been very excited about our experimentation with the pyramids. Kathy has had a long-established bed-wetting problem where I was changing sheets three times a night with complete exhaustion. Nothing had happened and I had hoped with all my heart that TM might help this. While TM has seemed to do absolutely amazing things, it did not affect in any way the bed-wetting routine or its frequency.

"I think it is important to note that obviously—and I don't know how to explain it—it isn't TM, and the only other thing I am doing is pyramids, and even if you don't believe in pyramids—when you don't have to get up out of bed three times a night to wash linens, you believe in God, or you believe in pyramids, or something—so I'm ever so grateful for this find, and I really think that if one has bed-wetting problems with children and would seriously follow this and keep daily records, they would find it to be of help. I've tried to convince some young parents, but apparently they are too young, but at least I'm satisfied that it has practically solved my problem, and if it isn't completely solved I'm not going to be concerned—it's so much better I can live with it."

What follows is Mrs. C.'s condensation of 173 entries in her log after Kathy had meditated for one year. It is best that the results are reported in Mrs. C.'s own words:

"We are excited about Kathy's results as we feel TM is a breakthrough for all handicapped and especially the retarded...All the following notations are tremendous advances considering Kathy's level and past history. They are extremely meaningful and prove the benefits of relaxation on the nervous system.

"Awareness, Alertness, Perception: Kathy never pays

any attention to the phone. After the fourth call I realized that each time it rang, Kathy called out 'Phone." I was fixing Sunday breakfast and Kathy was watching television. When the Catholic program is on, she turns to another channel. I did not notice what was on the screen until she told me to 'be quiet' and she then said a new word, 'Mass.' She had not switched the channel. Her glasses often make a sore behind her ear. She will never allow any type of padding under her glasses. This night she let me use a small Band-Aid and did not want to remove it in the morning. Previously while eating out, Kathy never took her eyes or action away from her plate. On this occasion she followed a couple out the door with her eyes and when she put her fork down and turned her head and stared at the humorous conversation at the next table, George and I almost fainted. Kathy came to me after eating, coughing and pointing to her mouth, saying a word I did not understand. She went to the sink and pointed to a watermelon 'seed.' This was the first time she was able to diagnose her own problem and tell me. Choosing a cotton blouse for her to wear, I said, 'I don't believe it needs ironing, it's okay to wear.' She shook her head and said, 'no,' and pointed to the iron. Never had an opinion before. We had a behavior problem at work (the work station where Kathy receives training). I brought her home and explained very carefully and emphatically that this was never allowed. The only punishment that is meaningful to Kathy is taking away her television. This brings tears every time. On this occasion I informed her that there would be no television for the rest of the day and night. No tears! She picked up a book and went to her room. I believe this was the first time she understood the punishment. I had borrowed six folding chairs. Kathy saw the chairs and heard me ask George to put them in the trunk of the car. Driving the next morning, I hit a chuckhole. While my mind was wondering what the noise might be in the back of the car, Kathy said, 'Chairs.' I often have hoarseness due to sinus. Our dressing conversation is fairly limited, i.e., 'take gown off,' 'hand me a towel,' etc. On this particular morning she looked in my face and asked, 'Cold?' Looking out the picture window at the bright sunshine, Kathy smiled and said, 'Nice!' First time to comment on good weather. Whenever we have dessert, I tell her that we are cheating. Kathy saw me cutting a second piece of pie and gave me a slight spanking (where I deserved it) and said, 'Cheating.' Showing us the television schedule, she said the word 'guest' and then pointed to the guest's name in the program description. I put a shirt on Kathy for the first time this season that has three mice hanging on cottontails. She smiled (remembering the shirt) and said, 'Mice.'

"Creativity: Kathy's counselor repeated three times that Kathy was doing a fantastic job. In seven years at the workshop the only comment I heard was that 'she does quite well.' The breakfast plates in our cupboard have sixteen smaller plates stacked on top of them. Kathy wanted a large plate and eased it out slowly, tipping and sliding smaller dishes off. Our car door sticks and she has seen me reach through the window and release the latch. She was able to do this without instruction or help even though this involved tremendous coordination for her— reaching and pulling straight out from herself. She provided spontaneous kitchen help by opening the cupboard, selecting the proper piece of Tupperware, and pouring into it a half can of peas which I had left out. Kathy never tolerated ice cubes in her drink. She put ice cubes in our drinks and now asks for ice in her tea. She became excited about the Christmas tree at the workshop. Said, 'Tree. Own.' So we put up a Christmas tree two weeks early for her benefit. Was never interested before. She now uses the belt reducer at the spa. Although she has some trouble getting in and out of it, it was impossible for her before. Kathy has never touched anything on the stove. Since last July she has been looking into the coffee percolator. With our new coffeemaker you cannot warm coffee over so I keep the percolator next to it. If the red light is not lit on the new coffeemaker, Kathy pours the coffee from one pot to the other. We have a birdfeeder in the yard but Kathy has never paid it any attention. On this day she pointed to herself and headed for the birdfeeder with dry bread.

"Tolerance: I told Kathy that it was time to meditate and then noticed that Santa Claus was on an old 'Lucy' re-run. I asked if she wanted to wait until it was over. To my utter amazement she stood up immediately and turned the television off and went downstairs to meditate. Removing a splinter from Kathy's finger has always taken two people. We were alone and both of my hands were busy with the magnifying glass and needle but Kathy held perfectly still until the splinter was removed. We went to a fish restaurant with a friend who enjoys a few beers before dinner. Dean is a great story teller and Kathy actually sat and listened and enjoyed him. At the end of the second pitcher of beer, I asked the waitress to bring Kathy's food. She was beautiful throughout the whole meal, never bugged us to hurry and never once said 'home.' Sunday Mass is generally forty-five minutes but Easter Sunday is special and we were in church for one hour and forty-five minutes. Kathy did not mention home or appear to be at all restless (the adults were). Last year we started Putt-Putt Golf and she did not appreciate my helpful hints. This year she was not grumpy, appeared to be listening and is doing better. Every six months we have a review at the workshop and Kathy sits in on this conference although nothing is directed to her. The counselor commented that this meeting was Kathy's best attendance on a tolerance level. Kathy is very short and all new slacks have to be shortened. This becomes a very irritating experience for both of us. George could not believe that we managed to mark two pairs of slacks without an argument.

"Socialization: Kathy came out of the television room and said 'Hi' to her brother-in-law. He was not paying attention to her but she proceeded to tell him 'plastic done—pink curlers,' bringing him up-to-date on her contract work. We had a beautiful day at a picnic. There was no repeating of 'eat—eat,' her prime interest. Swung in the rubber tube swings which she would never use before. Climbed up the standard-size slide; her first experience. At Bella Vista, Arkansas, our salesman turned around in the car and said, 'Hello, Kathy.' Immediately her hand came up in greeting. Previously she would have ignored him. At motels her only interest is television. Here she was delighted (big smile) over the sliding door out onto the porch. George took her picture and told her to smile. Kathy said, 'Cheese.' While eating in the television room, I held my one dish in my hand and sat coffee cup on the floor. When Kathy had only her coffee left, she pointed that I should put my cup on her tray and moved it between our two chairs. Attended a wedding at the church and Mass was about forty minutes. Then there was fifteen minutes in the reception line, followed immediately by another ten-minute wait in a cold, drafty hall waiting to speak to a woman I had not seen in thirty years; another wait in the food line and a delay in cutting and serving the cake! No problem at all. I would not have believed the evening if I had not witnessed it personally.

"Communication: I sent Kathy for the scissors in the dresser drawer. I asked if she had found them and she answered, 'Uh-huh, dresser.' When I comb her hair, I tell her it looks beautiful. On vacation George announced that it was a beautiful morning and Kathy repeated 'boo-oo.' The next morning Kathy felt I had spent sufficient time on her hair and told me it was 'boo-oo.' At bedtime she was a little grumpy and I said, 'Oh, come on, Kathy, be happy!' She repeated 'happy' and smiled, then yawned and said, 'Sleepy,' both new words. The dentist comment-ed that she had a pretty wristwatch. Kathy replied, 'Daddy watch.' Her father had bought a new digital watch for himself the night before. This was the first

communication with the dentist aside from 'yes' or 'no.'
The night before George's birthday I told Kathy that he
would be fifty-nine. At the spa the next day she told the
women, 'Daddy birthday—fifty-nine.' They were resur-
facing lanes at the bowling alley and she told her father,
'Bowling closed two weeks.' Voluntarily repeating a word
she hears is terrific but spontaneously using new words is
almost unbelievable for Kathy. She started using 'FBI'
instead of just 'I'; 'hungry' in place of just 'eat'; 'freezing'
instead of 'cold'; 'pop can is empty', not just 'gone';
'mayonnaise' pronounced very clearly; after twelve years
of bowling she started saying 'split'; watch was on
'backwards'; and after four years it is now 'Ames Bank',
not just 'bank'; and 'Ponderosa' has become 'Ponderosa
Steak House.'

"Interaction: We drove past Kings Restaurant. Kathy
pointed across the street to the television station and said
a word which I didn't understand. A few seconds later she
said, 'bowling.' Then I knew that the first word was
'Patrick,' a television sportscaster. Then she said, 'Kings
new.' Three days later I learned that Kings is the new
sponsor of a bowling program. Kathy has always had a
remarkable sense of direction. She tapped my arm while I
was driving, telling me to move to another lane preparato-
ry to making a turn in two or three blocks. Pointing to a
program in the *TV Guide,* she gestured like drinking. We
read of an alcoholic problem and asked if the woman was
an alcoholic. Kathy said, 'Yes.' We drink socially and she
could only have seen a drunk person on television. I
certainly did not realize that she knew the meaning of the
word. Showing us the *TV Guide,* she pointed down and
said, 'Car.' In the description Nancy Drew was in a plane
trying to spot a car on the highway. Watching 'Happy
Days,' three times during the program the father said
that if things did not improve, he was going to run away
to Tahiti. Later the mother announced to the children,
'Your father has run away!' Kathy laughed and turned
around and told me, 'Tahiti.' I was working at home and

had a sweater around my shoulders. Kathy pointed to it and asked, 'Cold?' She never comments about my clothing unless I am wearing something new. At spa Kathy was swimming with me supporting her. Two women said encouragingly, 'You're doing fine!' On the return lap, Kathy turned her head and told them, 'Bowling tomorrow—off Saturday.' Speaking to strangers was sufficient but trying to talk and swim at the same time was an accomplishment.

"Physiological: Whenever we asked Kathy to smile, she would turn her head upwards. Now she actually smiles. Kathy has never taken an interest in photographs. I opened an envelope of finished prints and was amazed to see Kathy beside me looking at the pictures. We were driving and she showed me the book marker. I said, '31,' and she repeated. She turned the page and I said, '32.' She continued counting and turning the pages and I repeated each number after her. Hearing my own voice at '65' I began to cry for joy. We continued up to '157,' the last page in the book ... 15 or 20 minutes of continuous speech! There have been sensitivity changes. She will now jerk her head when the Merthiolate makes contact. She burned her hand on the hot coffee pot and tried to blow on it. Her balance and coordination have greatly improved. She will now run in the snow and on ice. Before Transcendental Meditation she would not even walk in the snow. She now walks up and down escalators while the steps are moving. She lifted a large can from a high shelf while balancing another can on top of it. Kathy had a constipation problem for fifteen to twenty years; only one bowel movement per week, using an enema or suppository. After two months of meditation enemas or suppositories are never necessary and she is now having almost daily bowel movements. Kathy has never blown out a birthday candle. On this year's birthday she blew out the candles. She did not purse her lips but actually huffed the candles out."

In her report to us, Mrs. C. stated: "I am convinced in my own mind (George also) that Kathy's speech has definitely improved since she has been meditating in the pyramid. We are going to have her speech analyzed at our speech evaluation clinic, which is an exceptional facility. I would never have considered this without the latter development.

"My big excitement over pyramids is over the bed-wetting situation. To provide a little history on this problem, in February 1973 we began a program with Pacific International Limited—using the screen on the bed and a battery-bell which rings when the individual wets. This was a slow process but we were desperate and were afraid to go to medication which the doctor said had side effects. In March 1975 Kathy had a series of seizures in a few days and we began treatment with a neurologist. He felt she was grossly undermedicated and increased her phenobarb and added Dilantin. At this point she had no seizures for a one-year period but then for three years she had a pattern of several in one or two days. Was not happy with the medication but did not want the seizures to become more frequent. The bedwetting seemed to improve some but was replaced by releasing the bladder on the bedroom floor (which fortunately was tiled) or the side of the bed as she put her slippers on. I felt from the beginning that it was the Dilantin (new to her system) or the fact that she was drugged and not alert enough to awaken in time. I took her to a urologist, who found no problems. I finally convinced the neurologist that he could try taking her off the Dilantin. I hoped this would correct our problem. Both doctors said it was not an issue. Perhaps they were correct or perhaps it went from a cause to a habit. I had taken the screen (Pacific International) off Kathy's bed in June as it no longer served the need. I feel we had accomplished something with it but the floor elimination was a new problem. I have kept daily wetting charts since February 1973, but listed below are the nights in each month when wetting accidents occurred during the period from August 1975 through September 1976:

August 1975	5	March	5
September	3	April	8
October	8	May	9
November	6	June	8
December	2	July	3
January 1976	8	August	3
February	4	September	1

"We were on vacation during the early part of September 1976, were traveling and very fortunate in that we had only one accident during the month and this happened after we returned home.

"We had a wet floor incident on September 28, 1976. On September 29 we put pyramids under Kathy's bed. She knew what we were doing. Whether she understood or not, there is no way of telling—at least she did not object. I submit the following schedule for the period October 1976 through September 1977:

October 1976	0	April	1
November	1	May	0
December	2	June	2
January 1977	0	July	2
February	1	August	2
March	2	September	0

This table concludes an amazing report. It reveals a considerable change in control of physiological functions. Kathy's attending physicians told her parents that the condition was not of a physical nature, but was emotional, a signal of stress, etc. When Kathy became involved in meditation, she became more relaxed and several shifts evidently occurred. When the pyramids were added to the exercises, a more profound shift occurred in consciousness and consequently Kathy developed greater control over mental, emotional, and, in turn, physical functions.

Biofeedback scientist Dr. Paul Levine of Point Loma, California, has reported that during stress or anxiety skin resistance decreases. During transcendental meditation, however, skin resistance increases considerably, indicating deep relaxation, reduction of anxiety, and reduction of emotional disturbances. While most subjects show spindles in alpha waves during meditation the brain waves also show periods of beta spindles synchronized and in phase from all points of the scale.

(Brain waves are measured by an electronic instrument called an electroencephalograph. There are four principal waves produced by the human brain: delta, the sleep band; theta, a state of deep contemplation when the subject is unaware of his environment; alpha, an inner awareness state which indicates relaxation but also is conducive to problem solving; beta, a mental state in which the subject is alert to any stimuli. Spindles are bursts of activity as shown by ink marks on a script recorder.)

Dr. Levine also said transcendental meditation synchronizes electrical waves in the left and right cerebral hemispheres, bringing about coordinance of phase.

"This fact, together with the findings of increased intelligence, increased learning ability, and increased academic performance, may be interpreted as implying functional integration of the analytic and verbal skills of the left hemisphere with the synthetic and spatial skills of the right hemisphere," he said.

Kathy made gain on all these fronts after starting meditation, and on the basis of this integration the nervous system becomes more flexible and stable at the same time. It would seem that the right hemisphere of her brain started interacting with the left hemisphere to a greater extent than ever before.

Discussing the phenomenon of meditation in his chapter, "Consciousness and Quantum Theory," for

Edgar Mitchell's *Psychic Exploration,* physicist Dr. Evan Harris Walker stated: "...It is easy to see that if the demands placed on the brain's data-processing capacity by the individual's environment were relaxed, it would be possible to select a brainwide pattern of firing of the synapses that would greatly enhance the quantum mechanical interconnection mechanism. Such a pattern would be provided by a rhythmical firing of the synapses, forming an in-phase wave of synaptic excitations traveling through the brain, as with the alpha and theta brainwaves. Under these conditions, the consciousness could incorporate a large portion of the subconscious brain activity...There is, in addition, an enhanced or expanded conscious experience arising from the incorporation of a larger portion of the brain's activity into the ongoing conscious state..."

It seems safe to assume that Kathy was able by means of meditation to incorporate more of her subconscious and the intuitive consciousness of her right hemisphere within the functions of her left-hemisphere activities. Meditation assisted her in strengthening a bridge between her two worlds, which were only weakly interacting prior to this. Following our model that the physical body is an expression of the consciousness, when Kathy focused her attention away from her environment, which was anxiety-producing for her, and directed it inwardly, she became more in tune with states of mind in which she felt comfortable and thus "created" a more responsive brain, nervous system, and body.

The rational mind feeds upon stimuli from the outside. When the senses have little to stimulate them, the rational mind becomes less active and the inward-looking intuitive mind becomes more active. The rational mind, or the left hemisphere, apparently monitors the tardyon world of matter and the intuitive mind, or right hemisphere, monitors the tachyon world of antimatter. Sensory deprivation experiments involve placing an individual in a setting where there are no sights, smells, sounds, etc., to stimulate his senses. These studies have revealed that such conditions tend to inhibit the reasoning but greatly improve the intuitive and mystical skills. This is the purpose of bare, isolated cells used by Christian monks and the remote caves used by some Eastern ascetics. These individuals interact quite well with the reasoning, material world. They want to get in better contact with the spiritual domains. Kathy, on the other hand, likely feels quite comfortable with the intuitive dimensions of herself but needed to get in better contact with her environment and her reasoning mind. Meditation was used in both instances to build the bridge between worlds. In India, oftentimes the mentally retarded are held in veneration for it is believed they are in closer contact with the higher mind. That culture idolizes the intuitive levels of the mind, while our culture idolizes the agility of the reason.

In any case, meditation apparently has a great deal to offer in unfolding the human potential. Its uses as a therapeutic tool are rapidly expanding and Harold Bloomfield, Michael Cain, Dennis Jaffe, and Al Rubottom state in the book *What Is Meditation?:* "Preliminary reports suggest that meditation greatly speeds up the process of therapy, leads to deeper access into the psyche, and consistently gives better results than therapy without meditation. Its properties of relaxation certainly contribute to this, but in addition we suggest that some additional psychological properties of the experience of pure awareness affect the patients' ability to deal with highly frightening psychic material with a minimum of anxiety."

And in the chapter "Meditation Research: Its Personal and Social Implications" for *Frontiers of Consciousness,* Fred Griffith states: "The medical profession has shown interest in the possibility that meditation can help curb drug abuse and fight anxiety and hypertension, and educators have begun to explore the possibility that TM may be a valid addition to high school and college curricula. Linden's [W. Linden, "The Relation Between the Practicing of Meditation by School Children and Their Levels of Field Dependence-Independence, Test Anxiety and Reading Achievement," Ph.D. dissertation, New York University, 1972] study with third-graders has indicated that meditation may help decrease test anxiety among students, and meditation more generally seems to be a way of helping students improve their functioning and well-being..."

Kathy took another big step forward when she started meditating inside of a pyramid. Why would this occur? How could the pyramid contribute to her improved functioning?

In *The Secret Power of Pyramids* and *The Psychic Power of Pyramids* we described experiments with meditation inside of pyramids. We told how many people had related to us their experiences and how we discovered that several common experiences were being reported by people throughout the country. The commonalities included: 1) It seemed easier to meditate inside of a pyramid than in other settings; 2) even though the distractions were still imminently present—voices, traffic, phones, etc.—and hardly blocked by wood or plastic, still there was a distinct impression of being more removed from these distractions; almost as though the world outside had been moved to some distance away; 3) as external stimuli faded, the feeling grew of being enveloped in a comfortable and even benevolent field or force; 4) awareness grew of a presence but this seemed to be identified more as field than a personalized force; 5) frequently an internal flow of energy was felt and sometimes this was translated as a vibration; 6) the time warp—a complete loss of the sense of time; usually the time would seem much shorter than it had actually been; 7) a great deal of visual content, usually meaningful to the subject, and quite often geometrical and archetypal symbols would be part of the content. Because of these and other experiences, a number of people told us that they had progressed more in their meditation inside of pyramids than in other settings. Also, concentration and study were frequently reported as being easier while inside of pyramids.

If these were cases of just imagination, how can one explain the higher or mystical levels which yielded real advances in intuitive input, creativity, relaxation, tranquillity, insights, etc.? Why, instead of the commonality of experiences, wasn't there a vast array of unrelated matter? These cases cannot be so easily dismissed.

The heightened meditative experiences may be partly attributed to expectations and positive states of mind, yet these factors hardly explain the intensity of the experiences, including those of skeptical as well as novice individuals, the repetition, and the progress made by Kathy.

Earlier we explained that a growing body of evidence indicates that the human mind functions on two levels of existence. Part of the mind—probably operating through the left hemisphere of the brain—deals with the realm of matter, of sense perceptions and the reasoning upon these experiences. Another part of the mind—the right hemisphere—functions in the domain of the abstract, the non-physical, and outside the framework of space and time. The mind is a dweller on two planes, of matter and antimatter, and thus serves as the bridge or interface between worlds.

The mind can generate a measurable electromagnetic field and has been shown to exercise change on instruments, objects, plants, animals, and other humans. As an agent of change the mind can affect the body which it occupies positively or negatively. Psychosomatic medicine has clearly shown that one's mind can make one ill or it can make one well. These forces and changes take place within the tardyon world of the mechanical, chemical, and electrical.

Yet, the human mind apparently is not limited to these

forces. Part of its activity can penetrate any electromagnetic barrier; it can overcome gravity, and defy space and time. This portion of the mind would seem to operate in the tachyon world of negative space-time or antimatter. By means of such disciplines as meditation the awareness focuses its attention less and less on physical substance and more on non-physical existence.

The many varied experiments with pyramids have been conducted on metals, liquids, solids, organic and inorganic materials, plants, animals, and humans. There have been blind studies and even double-blind experiments. Human subjects have included persons of all ages, philosophies, states of health, and they have been receptive and extremely skeptical. Throughout it all there has been a consistent demonstration of an unusual force acting within the space of the pyramid whether it is two inches tall or house size. There is evidence to indicate that part of this force is electromagnetic in nature. To the extent that it is, some phenomena occurring inside of a pyramid can be duplicated by the application of electromagnetic fields to test objects and subjects. But some of the phenomena appear to occur in direct opposition to what we would expect from the known forces of nature. Yet these phenomena fit quite well within present theories concerning particles which move faster than the speed of light, in the domain of negative space-time.

If the pyramid does indeed slow down the tachyon in order to interact with particles moving at and below the speed of light—as discussed earlier—it can serve as the bridge between two worlds. The human mind dwells in both worlds, interacting with both physical and non-physical substance. It evidently receives and transmits electromagnetic particles, for we know that it responds to gamma rays, X-rays, ultraviolet light, various visible light bands, sound, radio waves, etc. Now the pyramid experiments would indicate that the human mind also interacts with non-physical particles—the world of the spirit, in religious traditions—or tachyon forces.

It well may be that the reason people are experiencing feelings of freedom, separation from the body, intuition, mystical or transcendental states, mental projection in which space is non-inhibitive, rejuvenation, time warps, impressions of spiritual presence, etc. is that all of these experiences appear to be beyond matter and space and time and belong on the other side of existence in the world of negative space-time. They tend to be enhanced inside of a pyramid because it presents a field rich in tachyon particles.

It is interesting to note that the rational mind engaged in the work of thinking utilizes great amounts of energy. Anyone who has spent several hours cramming for a final exam or grueling work over income taxes knows just how exhausting these mental exercises can be. This is the rational mind operating in the tardyon world and it requires energy for nourishment. As a matter of fact, the human brain claims first priority over our energy resources. On the other hand, the human mind engaged in meditation or contemplating inside of a pyramid gains energy, it is more rested than before the experience. It is said that when we sleep our awareness moves beyond our physical bodies to our ethereal bodies, or "life bodies," according to some traditions. This may be the reason that we are more rested after sleep than before as we have put ourselves during sleep in the position of obtaining tachyon particles.

The more energy we expend on our rational mind the more work it accomplishes. On the other hand it has been proved time and again that the harder one "works" at meditation or trying to move the needles in the right direction on biofeedback training machines the more one defeats oneself. In order to succeed with the intuitive mind, or the superconscious mind, one has to be inactive, i.e., receptive but passive. Again, this would follow as this mind functions just the opposite of the rational mind.

An interesting phenomenon occurs when a healer directs energy to a patient, when someone is using "mental power" to move a physical object or sending a telepathic message to a human receiver thousands of miles away. In these instances we seem to have some of our best examples of the mind serving as the bridge between two worlds. To add to the excitement, experiments reveal that the results are even more profound when they are performed inside of pyramids. This phenomenon is explored in the following chapter. It throws a new light on paranormal events and the pyramid saga.

SEVEN

Other Doors

We stopped at the bottom of the basement stairs and stared in amazement at the pyramid a few feet away. We had erected it three weeks before for the purpose of conducting studies in water treatment. It had not been used, however, because other matters had delayed our experiments. Nor had anyone been in the basement since that time as the upper levels of the house were under construction and the place was not occupied. The basement floor was damp, the result of heavy rains, and various insects scurried here and there.

But the floor on the inside of the large pyramid was covered with an assortment of dead crickets, water bugs, and other insects. Outside the pyramid only live insects could be seen.

Mention was made in *The Psychic Power of Pyramids* how insects appear to be repelled by pyramid energy. Food placed inside pyramids does not attract insects when left unwrapped. A friend of ours tried to attract ants from a colony near his outside pyramid with sugared milk. The ants swarmed over the milk placed outside the pyramid but were reluctant to enter the pyramid. A courageous member of the lot ventured inside but retreated before he reached the saucer placed in the middle of the pyramid.

What do these observations mean? What is so different about the space inside a pyramid that makes it either intolerable or fatal to insects? Are the frequencies or vibrations which appear to be beneficial to most plants, animals, and man too strong for the frail constitutions of insects? Or is there something about the force fields or frequencies which is intolerable to insects?

Several persons have told us that they are not bothered by mosquitoes while inside pyramids placed outdoors, even though there are ample openings through which they can enter. E. P. Benini told us that cockroaches were a big problem on his houseboat in the Bahama Islands, but he did not see a single cockroach in his pyramid studio built atop the boat.

Insects continued to be a problem inside one of the large pyramid homes, however. Yet the insects were always found on the east side of the pyramid and never on the west side. This would follow, according to our experiments with lasers, mentioned earlier, for the greatest amount of energy would be located on the west side of the pyramid.

The use of pyramids to eliminate insects has been successfully demonstrated by the United States Department of Agriculture. The following news item ran in the October 1977 issue of *The Kansas Farmer-Stockman:* "Maybe the pyramid shape does have magic qualities, as some people contend. USDA researchers have found that wooden pyramids painted white can be used to trap face flies and possibly other fly pests of livestock. In tests, 20 by 30 inch wooden pyramids reduced face fly numbers in pastures by 70 percent. Placed at a lower level, the pyramid attracted stable flies."

Normally we think of destroying insects by means of insecticides. Some ecologists and environmentalists, however, are resisting the widespread use of these poisons because of fear that toxins may remain in the soil, may find their way to water supplies, as well as food items, and prove fatal to bird populations which feed on the poisoned insects. Of late, a method has been discovered to eradicate insects without the use of insecticides. If this approach continues with the current rate of success, environmentalists will rest easier, farmers stand to save stacks of money, and the only ones holding the bag will be the producers and distributors of insecticides.

Meanwhile, those of us interested in learning more about known and unknown forms of energy may glean a few insights. We may be able to decipher why pyramids and insects don't mix.

An ingenious pest control specialist, Mike Sipe, of Palmetto, Florida, discovered about four years ago that he could rid a crop of insects by using them against themselves. He collected samples of the bugs, worms, etc. in his garden and ground them up. He diluted the juice with water and sprayed the mixture on his plants. Presto! Within three days the insects were either dead or had moved out.

A Florida farmer, Frank Batey, heard of Sipe's success and decided to give the process a try on his seventy-four acres of peanuts. He gathered up cabbage looper, stink bug, army worm, velvet-bean caterpillar, granular cutworm, and others and ground them in his kitchen blender. Batey then mixed about one half pound of the juice in three thousand gallons of water, enough to spray his entire crop.

According to the October 1976 issue of *Organic Gardening and Farming,* "So effective has the method been over two years that, in 1976, his third year, he didn't even have to spray the bug juice on his fields."

Batey reported that he had been spending about $2,000 a year for chemical pesticides on his land. In the first year of using the juice, the magazine said, Batey's average yield was about 5,300 pounds of peanuts an acre, compared to yields of 2,000 to 3,000 pounds reported by other farmers in Alachua County.

Sipe told the magazine that he believed three factors may be responsible for the dead bugs killing their uncaptured fellows: 1) Some of the pests in the collection are bound to contain viruses, bacteria, fungi, and other disease organisms that could trigger an epidemic among live bugs; 2) the odor of the solution, similar to the odor of a bug-infested field, may attract the pests' natural enemies; 3) the substances in the insects' bodies that trigger their responses to distress may be released in the blender and, in the spray, may repel the species once on the fields.

I (Schul) read the article and decided to try it on my potato patch, which had become badly infested with bugs. I gathered up a bunch and ground them in the blender while my wife was away from home, diluted the solution with four gallons of water, and soaked my plants. Three days later I couldn't find a live bug in the entire patch. A close neighbor followed suit and with equal results. We decided it couldn't be mere coincidence because potato plants can be quickly devoured by bugs if ignored.

In a follow-up article in the May 1977 issue of *Organic Gardening and Farming,* a number of entomologists and virologists are quoted as believing the process works because bug diseases are quickly spread in this manner. However, one story related in the article may throw a little different light on the subject. Dr. Lou Falcon, an insect pathologist at the University of California at Berkeley, related an incident in Nicaragua where he collected sick army worms. He identified a virus specific for army worm in the homogenate (the bug juice after grinding) and gave the spray to a farmer to use. "He applied it to his okra, which was infested with five different species of caterpillars besides the army worms. It cleaned them all up. I didn't believe it at the time and told him I thought he failed to clean the pesticide out of his spray equipment. But he insisted he'd cleaned the sprayer. This might have been the same effect Sipe has discovered," Falcon was quoted as saying.

This story may provide us with a clue to causes other than viruses for killing the insects or otherwise getting rid of them. If it was a matter of a virus specific to the army worm, why did it also wipe out the caterpillars? Going back to Sipe's third point, that the factor may be a substance triggering distress responses, we discover a connection between this incident and other research. A close look at these experiments may throw some light on what happens to insects in pyramid space.

A life signal may connect all creation. Polygraph expert Cleve Backster apparently demonstrated this when he elicited responses from plants when they were loved and when their well-being was threatened. Backster, an international authority on lie detector systems, shook up the scientific world when he hooked up a polygraph to a philodendron and demonstrated that the plant responded much like a human being experiencing various emotions. Knowing that humans react most strongly on the polygraph when their well-being is threatened, Backster wondered, "What would happen if I hurt the plant, if I burned its leaves?" At the very moment that he entertained this thought, the pen recorder jumped violently. That instant—with all of its vast implications—has now become a classic moment in the history of communications: It launched a host of experiments that were to demonstrate that all life forms are at some level in communication with one another. The mystic has contended for centuries that there is unity or oneness in the universe and he is apparently now being vindicated via the laboratory.

Theoretical physicist Dr. C. A. Muses was to say: "Absolute non-livingness appears increasingly to be an illusion, the answering reality to which is that there is no end of biology in some form, however far we look below us or however far beyond."

Backster was to find that his plants were in communication with other life forms and would record the moment that fertile eggs or brine shrimp were placed in boiling water. Plants, however, were not the only monitors of life's signals and he discovered responses occurred regardless how small or primitive the unit of life might be. This applied even to bacteria and he began to refer to this phenomenon as "primary perception below the cellular level."

The Wall Street Journal reported that Backster's experiments "seem to indicate that besides some sort of telepathic communication system, plants also possess something closely akin to feelings or emotions...They appreciate being watered. They worry when a dog comes near. They faint when violence threatens their own well-being. And they sympathize when harm comes to animals and insects close to them."

Backster proposes that an unknown kind of communication signal links all living things.

"The nature of the communication signal is somewhat mysterious," he told us. "It does not appear to be within the known frequencies and it does not take the form which can be shielded by ordinary means. I have tried to shield the plants with a Faraday screen—this prevents electrical penetration—and I've even used lead-lined containers. It would seem that the signal is not within any known portion of the electromagnetic spectrum, and distance does not seem to have a bearing."

Backster hypothesizes that the communication signal may be beyond the speed of light. In *Frontiers of Consciousness,* John White quotes Backster: " 'I'd like to get the space people to do something with a space probe to show that distance doesn't limit primary perception.' If possible he would put a plant wired to a polygraph on a space satellite and then station a person to whom it is attuned in Ground Control at Houston. Then he would cause the person to experience some unusual emotion—perhaps shock him with electricity—and have the polygraph data telemetered back to earth. That way the speed of propagation could be determined. 'I suspect,' he says, 'that this signal would return in half the normally expected time.' In other words, the time involved would be just what is normally required for the telemetric signal to travel from the space probe back to the receiving instrument, as if it had nearly instantaneously traveled from the person to the space-bound polygraph. 'If it did,' Backster says, 'you'd have evidence supporting a non-time-consuming form of communication, a phenomenon not falling within the electromagnetic spectrum, at least as we now understand it.'"

Dr. Harold Puthoff, a laser physicist at Stanford University, has suggested that the Backster effect may involve tachyons. He has been funded by Science Unlimited Foundation of San Antonio, Texas, to determine the nature of the mechanism involved in the communication system between living organisms. Using laser radar as a comparison signal with the Backster signal to get a comparative measurement on the velocity of propagation, the measurement would determine the time delay and reveal whether the signal is slower, equal to, or faster than the speed of light. If the speed is faster than light, tachyons would seem to be involved.

Not all scientists are in agreement with Backster's findings. Two scientists reporting at a 1974 seminar held by the American Association for the Advancement of Science claimed negative results in their efforts to replicate his work.

A number of other scientists, such as Marcel Vogel, senior chemist at IBM in San Jose, California, and Dr. Aristide Esser, a medical researcher at Rockland State Hospital in Orangeburg, New York, are strong supporters of Backster's work. Vogel told us that Backster's experiments led him into new fields of research and completely changed his life.

John White, mentioned earlier, asked Esser (who replicated Backster's findings that plants produce emotional responses) if some other explanation was possible for what he had observed. The answer was an emphatic no. "This is very simple," Esser told White. "You put an electrode on each side of a leaf, put a slight current on them and then measure the resistance. After things are stabilized, what you get as a readout on the pen recorder is a straight line with a little waving back and forth. Once you have this, you can tap at the leaf, blow on it, wiggle, even burn it—and nothing happens. But then if you take the owner of the plant or if you bring in somebody—but you don't let him know what you are doing—and you put him under pressure so he gets quite upset, all of a sudden the pen recorder begins to show tremendous deflections that are coincident with the time of giving the emotional stimulus to him. Immediately afterward, if you do any of the things you did before, nothing will happen. The deflections are synchronous with the stimulus emotion aroused in the person. So I don't see any possibility of them being artifacts because if that were so, you could find them at other times when the plant is hooked up but the owner isn't around. But we didn't find any."

Further evidence that there is a communications link between living organisms is being provided by research with Kirlian photography, or electrophotography, which uses electricity rather than light to expose photographic film. Pictures of radiation around living things such as human fingers, plant leaves, etc. have been produced by a number of researchers in this and other countries. Some of the most fascinating work in this field that we have observed has been done by two Wichita, Kansas, experimenters.

Clinical psychologist Dr. John Lester and professional photographer Jim Edwards demonstrated through hundreds of photographs that the amount of radiation surrounding a living thing corresponded directly to the health of the plant, animal, or human, and that as life ebbed away so did the radiations. Of particular interest were the interactions demonstrated through the radiations of plants to man, animals to man, plants to animals, and man to man. These interactions increased or decreased the amount of radiations depending on the type of influence. In taking pictures of an experimental rat in the process of dying, just before the moment of death a clearly defined distress signal emitted from the animal's brain.

A headline in the February 15, 1978, issue of the *Medical Tribune* reads, "Magnetic 'Halo' Leaks Brain's Top Secrets," and staff writer Elliot Richman states in the article: "A magnetic field produced by the human brain in response to a somatic stimulus has been detected for the first time, a team of scientists at New York University here has announced. In research performed at the university's Neuromagnetism Laboratory, physicist Samuel J. Williamson, Ph.D., and psychologist Lloyd Kaufman, Ph.D., have employed a superconducting loop maintained at liquid helium temperature to detect minute extracranial magnetic fields which, they feel, aid in elucidating the workings of the brain."

Several years ago Russian scientist Dr. Alexander Gurvich declared that "All living cells produce an invisible radiation." He claimed to have found rays—that he named mitogenetic radiation—coming from plants and he supposedly demonstrated that radiation from the tip of an onion root bombarded the side of another onion root and caused a marked increase in growth. The strange radiation increased the growth of bacteria and yeast also, but the energy reaction was stopped by glass. Ordinary glass filters out ultraviolet light. Quartz glass, on the other hand, allows ultraviolet rays to penetrate and when quartz plates were used reactions were not inhibited. Gurvich discovered mitogenetic rays coming from people and claimed that illness altered the radiation. He found that when a sick person holds yeast culture in his hands even briefly the cells are killed.

It is interesting to note that yeast culture grows very rapidly inside pyramids, almost as though an optimal environment was present for this growth, while bacteria producing deterioration in water, milk, vegetables, meat, etc. are reduced when exposed to pyramid space.

Gurvich's work was performed in the 1930s and seemed

to hold great promise for medicine, yet it faded when he failed to produce a theory. But his work was not forgotten. Currently, Russian biophysicists are taking another look at Gurvich's work. At Moscow University Dr. Boris Tarusov has found that plants modulate their light and radiate signals bearing certain messages, including advance warnings of disease. The Soviets have found that light waves appear to carry information from one group of living cells to another at a distance, and that this communication appears to be by means of the ultraviolet band. (We would suggest that this communication may be by way of tachyons.) They claim that illness can be transmitted by rays. If so, the implications are that health states can be programmed through radiation.

According to Sheila Ostrander and Lynn Schroeder in their *Handbook of Psychic Discoveries* Vlail Kaznachey-ev, Simon Shchurin, and Ludmilla Mikhailova carried out more than five thousand experiments demonstrating communication between cells by means of ultraviolet light. They placed two vessels with quartz bottoms end to end. Living cell colonies were put in each of the containers. They infected one colony with a virus, yet the second colony fell sick at the same time and died of the same disease. Something was transmitting a sickness pattern to the healthy cells, but since the vessels were sealed, the scientists reasoned that the carrier would have to be some kind of radiation.

Working at the Institute of Clinical and Experimental Medicine at the U.S.S.R. Academy of Sciences, the three scientists extended their explorations. They used quartz containers and each time killed one colony of cells with radiation, viruses, or chemical poisons. Each time the unaffected cells also died. Yet, when the cells were separated by ordinary glass, which filters out ultraviolet light, only the treated colony was affected.

While this work and some of the other experiments mentioned suggest that a signal is carried by means of ultraviolet radiation, other frequencies may be involved.

Some glass and other materials may not only filter ultraviolet but other rays as well. It is known that quartz placed under pressure emits a piezoelectric charge. In *The Secret Power of Pyramids* we mentioned that the ceiling of the King's Chamber of the Cheops Pyramid consists in part of huge piezo quartz-bearing slabs of stone. It has been suggested that the builders used quartz in order to produce some kind of electrical charge or radiation within the chamber. This may be the case but there is also the possibility that quartz somehow enhances or amplifies an existing force.

The signal, however, may travel on a carrier wave beyond the electromagnetic spectrum. Soviet physicist Dr. Victor Adamenko has stated: "Experiments appear to show that plants receive some kind of emanation at a distance of a hundred miles and that known methods of screening from electromagnetic waves do not prevent the plant from receiving the signal."

If the signal cannot be filtered out then we may be looking for something more or in addition to ultraviolet light as a carrier wave. Many researchers are looking to psychic fields and different types of energy for explanations, while others are looking at quantum mechanics, and even tachyons. Tachyons become more and more attractive as certain types of phenomena continue to elude the laws of particles traveling at or below the speed of light.

Some of the unusual phenomena which refuse to conform with the known laws of our positive space-time world include levitation, telepathic communication (with both the sender and receiver shielded from electromagnetic radiation), thoughtography (implanting a mental image on film, even with an electromagnetic barrier between the subject and the camera), and the bending of spoons, keys, etc. by other than physical force. The latter phenomenon, popularized by the young Israeli Uri Geller, has become so common that it is now referred to as the "Gellerian effect." This phenomenon cannot be explained by what is known of electricity, magnetism, gravity, and so on. Spoons have been bent while sealed in vacuum-tight and electromagnetically shielded containers and over considerable distances.

At this point in time the most logical place to look for answers appears to be on the other side of the coin, in the domain of antimatter and negative space-time. In the world of positive space-time matter cannot just disappear, but dematerialization is perfectly acceptable where antimatter reigns. Geller, according to many carefully conducted experiments, can make objects disappear and reappear, oftentimes at some distance. Although Geller and others performing the same feats apparently do not understand how the phenomenon occurs, it would seem they are applying the forces of matter for materialization and the forces of antimatter for dematerialization.

In *The Secret Power of Pyramids* and *The Psychic Power of Pyramids* we discussed the improbability of the builders of the Great Pyramid using crude instruments and manpower to lift and fit the huge stones in place. Some researchers have suggested that the builders used the principles of levitation, and even the highly respected Stanford physicist Dr. W. A. Tiller has speculated on that possibility. He has explained that levitation, rather than gravity, would apply in negative space-time.

While ideas regarding antimatter, negative space-time, and psi phenomena may seem somewhat foreign to us in our everyday world of vapors, liquids, and solids, it might be well to remember, as Buckminster Fuller has pointed out, that ninety percent of what is happening in human activity and interaction within nature occurs in realms of reality utterly invisible, inaudible, unsmellable, untouchable by presently developed human senses and must be relayed to us by instruments.

That world of invisible forces is with us each moment of our lives. Not only is gravity taken for granted but it would be difficult to imagine life without it. We have become so accustomed to electricity that we give it little thought beyond looking for the nearest plug-in. We know that light waves, magnetic fields, and radio waves permeate our environment and that when we turn on a radio or television set we are not creating these waves but only making use of their presence. They are not only with us every second, they are also passing through our bodies. Our bodies themselves are electromagnetic fields and have their own frequencies. Recent studies reveal that the cells of our bodies, our organs, glands, etc. have their own frequencies or rate of vibration, as does the body as a whole. Kirlian photography, acupuncture, sensitive voltmeters, force field detectors, photomultipliers, and brain wave monitors have made us aware of the electrical nature of the human body. These instruments and techniques have demonstrated that the human body is a generator and capacitor of electromagnetic fields. Further, the body is a transmitter and receiver of radio waves. As part of these force fields, the human system influences and is influenced by all of the frequencies in its environment...and that environment apparently is extended to some distance.

To what extent do we affect things in our environment? Are we radiating a force field that is generated by our physical bodies, our emotions, our thoughts—most of which are on unconscious levels—which influence everything about us? Is it possible to make even a simple observation without allowing that the act of observing changes the object under examination? Clearly, dowsing for water, for example, requires the dowser to be part of the circuitry. This seems obvious. It is equally obvious that the human subject is part of the circuitry in biofeedback experiments. The electroencephalograph—an instrument used to measure brain waves—is not going to make pen marks on the graph paper until the subject is linked into the circuitry. The human is the bridge between the pen marks and the instrument.

But the human input is difficult to measure. It varies widely between individuals and with the same person from time to time, depending on what he is responding to—health, sickness, anger, contentment, anxiety, etc. If there are qualities of energy emanating from the human system, it would seem that these fields can be attributed to all persons. More than likely this is true. However, there appears to be a vast range in the strength of the human transmitter and receiver. Some people can allegedly heal with their hands while others cannot. Some people can affect the growth of seeds and have what we call "green thumbs," while others do not have or have not developed these skills. Some people can dowse for water, bend spoons, voluntarily adjust their heartbeats and skin temperatures, etc., while others fail in these tasks.

A growing mountain of research findings indicates that the experiment can never be completely isolated or measured apart from the experimenter. Let's take a brief look at the work of one of these researchers, Marcel Vogel, mentioned earlier:

After convincing himself that Backster's work was worth investigating, Vogel discovered that he could affect the deterioration rate of leaves severed from a plant. One leaf he ignored and it dehydrated and turned brown, while another leaf he kept green and fresh by willing it to remain so.

An internationally recognized expert on liquid crystals, Vogel wondered if the "psychic energy" which kept a leaf alive could affect liquid crystals. He took hundreds of color slides of liquid crystal behavior magnified three hundred times. He concluded that crystals are brought into a solid or physical state by pre-forms or ghost images of pure energy which anticipate the solids. As plants could pick up the intentions of humans, so Vogel was equally convinced that intent produced some kind of energy field.

To demonstrate the role that he personally played in his experiments, Vogel hooked two plants to the same recording machine. From the one plant he tore off a leaf and the second plant responded to this "hurt"... but only when Vogel paid attention to it! It became clear to Vogel that a certain state of consciousness on his part was an integral part of the circuitry in monitoring his plants.

Vogel tells his audiences that a life force, or cosmic energy, surrounding all living things is sharable among plants, animals, and humans. "It seems," he states, "that I act as a filtering system which limits the response of the plant to the outside environment. I can turn it off or on, so that people and plant become mutually responsive. By charging the plant with some energy within me, I can cause the plant to build up a sensitivity for this kind of work. It is extremely important that one understand that the plant's response is, in my opinion, not that of an intelligence in plant form, but that the plant becomes an extension of oneself..."

This position highlights the difference in approaches between Vogel and Backster. Vogel is concerned with the human control of the plant whereas Backster contends that his plants, left alone, will quite normally react to their environment. Quite possibly they are both correct to some degree. But the question one immediately raises to Backster's position is whether an experimental plant is ever alone. It may be that plants not under human scrutiny react to their environment without any help from human beings. Yet there is no way that we can measure this interaction because the moment we become interested in the matter we have contributed to the action.

Speaking of researchers who have endeavored to elicit electrical responses from plants and other living organisms by means of emotional and mental stimuli, Vogel has stated: "Hundreds of laboratory workers around the world are going to be just as frustrated and disappointed as these men until they appreciate that the empathy between plant and human is the key, and learn how to establish it. No amount of checking in laboratories is going to prove a thing until the experiments are done by properly trained observers. Spiritual development is indispensable. But this runs counter to the philosophy of many scientists, who do not realize that creative experimentation means that the experimenters must become part of their experiments."

Where does this leave us in our experiments with pyramids? In the same place where everyone else is ... as personally involved, as much of the circuitry as is the physician with his patient, the botanist with his plants, the zoologist studying animal behavior, the biologist peeking at his microorganisms. All of us are factors in our equations; we cannot study our subject without studying ourselves.

Pyramid research presented us with the dilemma of not being able to explain the unusual results by means of the usual laws of nature. These qualities simply did not appear sufficient to explain everything that was happening inside pyramids.

Some have asked if we are dealing in magic. Well, we are, of course, but not in the sense in which the questions are asked. Magic has been a much misunderstood term. When most people think of magic, they either envision the stage magician doing his bag of tricks or they imagine someone working with strange supernatural forces. But magic in its original definition had to do with the knowledge and application of natural laws. As magic was concerned, however, with those subtle laws of the universe dealing for the most part with the non-physical or invisible dimensions of life, they are considered by the less knowledgable as strange, miraculous, or, more often, as unreal. Magic doesn't depend on matter or substance but on form, on patterns. So does art, music, psychology, religion, etc.

As the new physics plunges us deeper and deeper into the subtler forces of nature and into what has become known as field theory, we find that what was once described as magic fits in nicely with the current understanding of energy and its various levels of expression. We, too, found that pyramid results depended to some extent on pattern rather than substance, not because we were seduced by magical spells but as a consequence of careful observation of experiments.

The symbol may well be the object in the final analysis, and pyramids may work because in a sense they are symbols of the Great Pyramid. We feel more comfortable, however, with the thought that certain laws apply to both big and little pyramids because of their mutual attributes. Pole or uncovered pyramids may work because the pattern remains, and some are now even claiming that pyramids created by laser beams or even correct mental projection produce results. They may work, for thoughts are things, according to some physicists. We are not arguing with these ancient and ultramodern views. What we are saying, however, is that pyramids of both substance and non-substance must be considered. As explained earlier, the pyramid appears to exist in both worlds.

We have echoed the words of some of the world's leading scientists, such as Mitchell, Vogel, Puthoff, et al., that the observer can no longer be divorced from that observed. If true, the principle would also apply to pyramid experimenters. We propose, however, that there are levels of involvement and that the pyramid is less closely linked to the experimenter than, say, the dowser is to his divining device. Clearly, the pendulum or the forked stick is not going to work unless the operator has hold of it; neither is a pair of pliers, a violin, or a microscope.

We are not denying that the experimenter is part of the pyramid's circuitry, but we propose that there are overriding forces at play which have established an optimal level of functioning for the pyramid. The force cannot be amplified, as our experiments revealed. Regardless of how negative, depressed, or skeptical the experimenter, the results produced by the experimenter were not appreciably altered.

The forces at play in pyramids seem to come under the domain of higher powers than our own. They continue to work in a more or less consistent fashion regardless of how charitable, selfish, fatigued, energetic, hostile, or kindly we happen to be on a given day. It is comforting to find that the laws behind pyramid phenomena apparently are not governed by the whims of imperfect man. If we are more deeply involved in the circuitry than we imagine, then it must be our higher selves at work, for we have never experienced, nor are we aware of any incidents, where the pyramid has been used by an individual to his own detriment or that of others.

It is fascinating to discover that there is not one thing in the universe which can be examined in isolation, regardless of how shielded or protected it may be. All of the vast forces of the universe are involved in all the smallest and seemingly inconsequential activities of nature. The more we learn about bugs and plant leaves and galaxies, the more we learn about pyramids. We would like to believe that the reverse also holds true.

EIGHT

Modern Pyramid Dwellers

"I WOULD say that the biggest change that comes over you, living in a pyramid house, is the spiritual change"..."Almost everyone who enters our home feels as though it is a spiritual place"... "The thing that you really notice is that you have more energy"... "Your rate of healing is so much faster than ordinarily"... "I've noticed that she is much happier as a person"... "All of your senses are enhanced"... "Your thoughts are brought one to one with your physical body..."

The dwellers within pyramid homes can provide us with unparalleled insights into pyramid energy. They are our pioneers, although they may not envision themselves as such, for they have passed through a door to what is still largely an unknown. They have invested their time, energy, and money in the belief that a pyramid home will be better than some other-shaped dwelling. It has been said by some of the world's great teachers that at some level, some state within all of us, we truly know. Do Gary and Debbie Noble know? Do Ed and Marilyn Buxton know? What kind of knowledge, conscious or unconscious, or what kind of stirrings, prompted them to these decisions?

Who can tell us more? Isn't this really the acid test? Or, as they say in our neck of the woods, the time has arrived to fish or cut bait. In many ways the pyramid home is the ultimate laboratory in this field of research. With pyramid homes we have the opportunity to observe the effects on people who are constantly exposed to pyramid space over long periods of time. Assuming that they do not sell their homes and move away, they will remain as experimental subjects for all the world to see through the days and nights, the months and the years ahead. Not only are we privy to the lives of people living inside pyramids but we also have the opportunity to observe the effects on a variety of materials, food storage and preservation, indoor plants, and most likely pets.

In *The Secret Power of Pyramids* and *The Psychic Power of Pyramids* we told of various buildings constructed in the traditional pyramid shape and we mentioned that some homes were under construction. Only now, however, has a sufficient amount of time elapsed for us to consider what the effects of pyramid living might be. Those individuals—such as the Nobles and Buxtons—

The Noble pyramid home near Coyle, Oklahoma. From left, Gary Noble, Debbie Noble, Ed Pettit, and Eva Noble (in front).

who are kind enough to share their experiences with others do so because they wish to contribute to whatever knowledge can be gained. All of us interested in pyramids have a great deal for which to thank them. They feel very good and positive about their futures and, as the reader will discover, they have no regrets. It will be exciting to keep in touch with them through the years—as I'm sure we will—and to watch what impact their lives have on others, and their homes on the construction industry.

We could tell of their experiences, what they've learned, etc., but it is much more fascinating to hear their stories as only they can tell them.

By way of background to Gary and Debbie Noble's account: They are in their middle to late twenties and they have one child, four-year-old Eva. Gary is a musician and Debbie is a biology teacher.

The home stands on rolling wooded land north of Oklahoma City, Oklahoma. It features a dozen rooms in its 2,193 feet of living space. It sits on a Cruciform foundation and the square base measures fifty-six feet on each side. It stands thirty-seven feet tall from the base to the apex. The ground floor includes two bedrooms, one in the southeast corner and one in the southwest corner, dining room, living room, bath, and kitchen. The master bedroom is located at the level of the King's Chamber on the second floor and is directly beneath the apex. The apex of the pyramid is equipped with skylights.

"The rooms are all built on angles and there's not a square room in the house except for the rectangular entryway," Gary told us. He added, "with a self-supporting roof and a double A-frame type of design, the house will offer less wind resistance and structurally will be about fifty percent stronger than most conventional homes."

To get to the Noble home one leaves the paved highway and turns into a picturesque country road. It is cattle country and few homesteads interrupt the flow of rocky grassland amply endowed with cedar trees. One sees the home at some distance before arriving. As one tops a hill, it is suddenly there, rising above the trees on its plateau, and there is something beautiful but startling about this experience. One has expectations as to how it will look but one is not quite prepared. Maybe it is its size, larger than one envisions, or perhaps its isolation, but one gets the distinct impression of having located a shrine. This awe remains as one draws closer. The mystique deepens as one learns how the pyramid came about and the unusual means of determining its location.

"The design for the house came to me through meditation," Debbie told us. "I had been meditating on my purpose in life and I asked what would be the most beneficial thing that I could do for my family. The answer I received was that I should build a pyramid home.

"I asked during my meditation where I could find this special spot on which the pyramid was to be built. I mentally saw myself going down a road, over a river, up a dirt road, and then I saw broad pastureland with cedars. I drew it all out on a piece of paper, but I didn't know where to look. Two days later a man called me, whom I had known, but I just never dreamed he would be willing to sell some of his land. 'Debbie,' he said to me, 'I don't know why but I have decided to sell the back part of my acreage. I decided to call you first.' I said I wanted it, but the one thing that bothered me was that the entrance to his land was not the one I saw myself driving down, so I still couldn't understand it. When we got out there, he took us on a different road than the entrance to his home..." Debbie paused, glanced inquisitively into our eyes, and added with a smile, "This road was the same one I saw in my meditation! There was the road, the river, definitely the land. When it was surveyed we learned that there were thrity-three and one third acres in the piece. That particular number has a special meaning to me so I know that the land was special.

"We walked around the land and found this place where it just kept drawing us. We would go in circles and

Looking upward to King's Chamber area in Noble home.

land back at this spot every time. We knew this must be the spot. It was a clearing with cedar trees surrounding it but we had to move only one tree. We needed a water supply and I knew there must be water here because young cottonwoods were growing here. So we took a witching stick and that's how we found our water supply...and it was pure water with a flow of twenty-two gallons per minute. We discovered that there was an underground river right beneath the pyramid. We plan to build a pyramid over our wellhouse. That way it will energize the water in the water tank."

We asked Debbie about their experiences since moving into the house and without hesitation she replied, "I would say that the biggest change that overcomes you living in a pyramid is the spiritual change. My whole life has been spiritually oriented, but it seems to me that you notice everything has become more purified; you notice how life is and you notice the energy of life. You understand what life is and that is very overwhelming. Also, people who come to our house feel spiritually affected. Almost everyone who comes here feels as though it is a spiritual place, a very spiritual place." You could feel the quiet reverence in her voice as she spoke. "When you pray, your prayers are answered; you receive a response to your prayers. You can feel an immediate one-to-one feeling of contact with, you know, the Heavenly Being. You feel as though your home is really protected and that everything you do is guided. It feels as though your whole purpose in life was known before you were born and that everything you have done is leading up to that purpose and it is being fulfilled."

It was important that we understand. Debbie felt what she was saying very deeply. One could read it in her face and in the quiet firmness of her voice. All of us fell silent and in those hushed moments the presence of the pyramid was everywhere, enveloping us, permeating our being. Outside the cedars stood, responding slowly to a slight southerly breeze, and somewhere among them a meadowlark called to its mate... not so different than anywhere else, but within these walls—rushing upward to the apex radiating in the sunlight—we seemed momentarily suspended in a special time and place. We could have remained thus transfixed for some time, but we finally interrupted the reverie to ask what their health experiences had been.

"Since I teach at school I am always around people who have all kinds of contagious diseases," Debbie told us. "When you do come in contact with those who are sick, you may get something like a cold. But the thing that you really notice is that it heals remarkably faster. Your rate of healing is so much faster than ordinarily. You really notice that you have more energy. You feel younger; you feel so young. In fact, the comment that I receive so many times from people is that they can't believe I am twenty-seven. They think I'm maybe twenty years old. I think it really has helped. It takes you to a point where you feel the best and then it keeps you right there and you don't change that much...

"But, as far as small children are concerned, it isn't that they stay at that age. They keep on growing normally. In fact, it seems as though it balances one's metabolism. My daughter was very small for her age when we moved into the pyramid, and no matter how hard I tried I couldn't get her to gain weight; she was really thin. Since we've moved into the pyramid, I haven't even had to worry about it. She has been growing very rapidly, almost to the point where she is caught up with normal growth. I have been keeping a record, and she had very fast growth when we first moved and now she has grown three and a half inches. She has been putting on weight and she keeps it on...

"I've noticed that she is a lot happier as a person. She has become really secure and very stabilized for her age. She sleeps all alone downstairs and is not frightened at

North side of Noble pyramid house.

all by it. Eva loves the pyramid and, in fact, I think children are much more aware of the energy. They can understand it more because they are open and they don't close their minds to it. She really is aware of it. If she has a cut or bruise, she wants to come up to the King's Chamber and sleep with us because she knows it will heal faster. She really believes it and I think one of the main things about healing is to believe that you can do it and especially in the pyramid. It helps you because it enhances your mind powers."

After we discussed the healing phenomenon as it occurs within the pyramid, how and why it may occur, and after we related some of the more interesting cases, the conversation drifted in the direction of unusual and curious things which people have experienced within pyramid space. This prompted Debbie to tell us about experiences that she and Gary had with a star or some other luminary object in the sky. We might speculate as to the nature of what they saw but, then, we didn't see it so it is really their story. Debbie and Gary are not sure. Whatever it may have been, they believe their experience is interesting and meaningful. We include it here in that same spirit and offer it as another account of experiences occurring to people living within pyramid homes.

"We definitely do have some experiences in the pyramid that do seem... interplanetary. I'll put it that way," Debbie explained. "I can't say whether it is a star, planet, UFO, or what this particular thing is, but I have friends who have also noticed it. The star seems real close to the house and when at night—every night—when you lie in the King's Chamber you can see it out of the northeast window. Gary and I have compared the movements—it's so amazing—that it's going right, going left, up or down, and it goes clear across the whole window... moving in almost a hypnotic way. It is very hypnotizing. The colors seem to fluctuate. They change between red and green and blue, almost like a hypnotizing pattern, but it's very comfortable. It's not frightening.

Front left, Ed Pettit, Bill Schul, and Tom Garrett at pyramid house near Coyle, Oklahoma.

When we first saw it, we were kind of leery; you just don't know what to expect. The more familiar it became, because it was there every night, we started looking forward to seeing it. You focus on it, almost meditate on it, and it almost draws you out of your body. You can almost tell that someone is talking to you, telepathically, of course, and it's like they are asking you if you would like to go. But if you say no, it is immediately gone. This is completely a voluntary thing; it's nothing to be frightened of because it is completely up to you. But the thing is, it almost draws you out of your body, like when you are meditating and you leave your body...that same sensation. When you stare out of that window, the walls—it is really strange—but they become as though they are transparent. You can see the layers of the wall but instead of seeing one solid wall you see twelve walls but you can see through them all. It's a really strange feeling but it's really neat.

"The star comes every night but it moves around. Sometimes you can see it out of a side window, but it moves around drastically, and that's the reason I can't believe it is an ordinary star. It's very bright. It's tremendously brighter than any other star...It will be there in the morning. It is silvery light but we can see it even though it is daylight and no other star is visible."

We spent little time discussing food items, for Debbie and Gary seemed more interested in talking about their experiences with the pyramid as people. They did say, however, that food was preserved longer and remained edible even though it dehydrated. Debbie pointed out that their tomatoes hadn't lasted long without dehydrating but even so were good on the inside. She noticed that her tomatoes turned from a red to an orange and she wondered if this was due to a loss of acid. We replied that we didn't know but that it would be worthwhile finding out.

"Food tastes a whole lot better inside the pyramid," Debbie said. "I've really noticed that all of one's senses are enhanced, especially the sense of hearing. At night when you turn everything off, you can actually hear the sound of the energy. It's almost like a buzz. When we first moved in, my daughter said, 'Mother, there is a bee buzzing in my ear!' It was the energy because that's exactly what it sounds like. It's a high-pitched buzz, but it has to be quiet inside the pyramid to hear it."

We related how other people sitting or meditating

inside of smaller pyramids had called our attention to this sound. Some, as with Debbie, had referred to it as a buzz, while others said that it was like a high "AUM." It is not uncommon for people to "hear" radar, a phenomenon mentioned of late in some scientific journals. All energy has a vibration and it may be that very sensitive people are able to pick up on this activity. Some people acquaint the vibration more with feeling than hearing, and quite a large number of people are able to see the energy fields around humans and sometimes other life forms.

Debbie explained that their exposure to the pyramid seemed to enhance their senses to the point where they are now much more sensitive to sound, touch, etc. Gary is a musician and he has a great deal of expensive recording and sound equipment in his home and they were excited about their experiences with music.

"You get a sound recording," Debbie said, "that has a beautiful chamber effect that you can't get naturally. It seems as though your creativity is so enhanced. When you play in here, it is totally different. Music has some link with the pyramid and I think you can achieve more with music inside the pyramid than you could ever hope to anywhere else. Your thoughts are brought one to one with your physical body so that you can control your voice. I've taken up singing and Gary's playing has just gotten out of this world. Really remarkable. And I totally think that it is the pyramid that has drawn this energy out of the air. There is the music of the universe which everything is tuned into. I feel that once you are in the pyramid you can tune into the music of the universe. It's like meditating. A lot of musicians try to tune into that music and to duplicate it, and that's very hard."

Gary described his sensations while playing inside his pyramid home as "like I'm in outer space. The music just comes out. It's like you leave your whole body and something else comes in and takes over and creates it for you. That's what's so tremendous about it. You are like an instrument and the words and music come through you."

"Your eyes also become tuned in," Debbie told us, "so that you can see so much better, almost microscopically. I teach biology and we do a lot of work with microscopes studying microscopic organisms. Now...I almost see those things without the microscope because I can tune my eyes into them. For instance, looking at a plant, I can see the cellular structure where I couldn't see it before."

Gary, Debbie, and Eva Noble have launched themselves on quite an adventure and one that may hold vast implications for themselves and many others. It is doubtful that they would trade places with any other three people in the world. Each day is a new adventure for them, one that they approach with enthusiasm and open arms. Will the rest of us some day despair of our cube-like enclosures and follow suit?

Buckminster Fuller, scientist, mathematician, author, architect, educator, and inventor of the geodesic dome, told us a long time ago that homes, offices, churches,

Pyramid church in Houston, Texas.

whatever, should be other than cube shape. As the years pass and more people build and live in other than cube-shape structures—mainly, the pyramid shape, we believe—it will be interesting to compare their spiritual, mental, and physical growth and well-being with those of others. Undoubtedly, we have much to learn about pyramids, about shapes in general, for that matter, and energy fields. What we propose now we may not be defending a decade from now, but judging from the experiences of those who have now lived inside pyramids for a period of time, they would appear to have made wise choices. Fuller speaks of harsh angles such as we have with cube-shape rooms and buildings where walls, floors, and ceilings are set at ninety-degree angles to each other. Recent studies with light, radio beams, and other electromagnetic fields and our investigations with tachyons indicate that right-angle structures may create interference waves which in colliding may establish resonances which are not beneficial to man, animals, and plants.

Practically all existing buildings, of course, have either cube-shape exteriors or cube-shape rooms and usually both. If we learn that other shapes are preferable, it would still be many, many years before these buildings could be replaced. Few of us living in cube-shape homes can afford to tear them down and start over. But there may be some solutions less dramatic and expensive which will provide us with some of the benefits of the pyramid shape.

Some benefits may be derived from roofs which are peaked rather than flat. This does not provide us with a pyramid, of course, but it is a prism, and those who read *The Psychic Power of Pyramids* will recall that Jack Dyer's plant growth study revealed that the prism produced growth second to the pyramid but in excess of other shapes. Experiments could be conducted using miniature prototypes of various house plans. Plants and small creatures, for example, could be used and various tests taken. Peaked roofs may have additional benefits other than shedding of rain and snow. Experiments could also be designed to measure differences in the roof angles, compared to conventional homes with roofs slanted to the correct pyramid angle. Should such experiments demonstrate significant differences, it would be less drastic to alter roof lines than rebuild entire homes.

Even this, of course, can be a problem for many people who cannot afford to remodel roof lines or for those people living in apartments and condominiums. Fortunately, however, pyramid structures large enough to sleep and meditate in are not difficult or expensive to build. Even smaller pyramids can be effectively used to treat and preserve food, treat water, and so on.

If one is sufficiently interested, there are ways to take advantage of the pyramid shape.

E. P. Benini lived on a houseboat in the Bahamas. Originally from Italy, he is a painter who lived and painted in the islands for thirteen years. He has just recently moved to Florida. Benini read our books and became so interested in pyramid power he decided to build a pyramid on top of his houseboat. Sleeping areas were located on the northwest and southwest and his studio was placed in the center of the sixteen-foot-square structure.

"Since I started painting in it," Benini wrote us, "there has been a tremendous change in my life. From a very practical and materialistic outlook on life I have changed to a life of research into the spiritual, a search for truth through philosophies, finally channeling my studies into the metaphysical and theosophy. As a result, my paintings have developed from studies on the nude to studies into the mind and higher planes. Success (financial) has also improved a great deal as the quality of my patience constantly evolved.

"Whether this is due to my aging or to the benefits of pyramid power, I do not know.

"On a more practical side, I can definitely state that in two years I have never found a cockroach inside the

William Mayfield's twin-pyramid home near Colorado Springs, Colorado.

pyramid, while I have a constant problem inside the perfectly sealed lower trailer. The shape of the pyramid acts as a stabilizer on the boat. I have been through various storms with winds up to eighty-five miles per hour without any rocking or damage.

"The pyramid is air-conditioned because of the tropical heat and humidity, but when it is not in operation plants kept in it grew twice the size of the ones inside the lower part of the boat with the same amount of light condition.

"On the negative side, I always found it uncomfortable to sleep in the bed until I moved the mattress on the floor in the center. The same was experienced by my various house guests, particularly by a psychic friend who woke up in a cold sweat and with a choking feeling.

"Also, the boat has never been broken into even when it stays empty for weeks at a time when I travel, while all the other ones at one time or another have experienced great losses."

Benini sold his houseboat to a couple "whose main reason for the purchase was to experiment with living with the pyramid." On his new property in a wooded area, Benini plans to build a large pyramid for his studio and for meditation purposes. He has also made a number of pyramid-shaped birdfeeders.

William Mayfield has lived in his pyramid house since October 1, 1976. Located near Colorado Springs, Colorado, with the Rocky Mountains looming on the west, it is a "picture postcard"setting.

"I finished my pyramid home in October, and I am really excited about it," Mayfield wrote us. "It works! It has just been super, and it is getting better every day...I have done a lot of experiments in the house and they all work. But the most exciting thing to experience is the wonderful feeling of excellent health. The energy within the house is very noticeable. I just don't want to leave the place."

Mayfield and a partner own Design Group Architects and Two's Company Builders, Inc., 1624 S. 21st Street, Colorado Springs, Colorado 80904. Mayfield designed

Entrance to Mayfield's twin-pyramid home.

and constructed his pyramid home and he and his partner now furnish plans for custom pyramid houses. Actually, the home consists of two connected pyramids, each twenty-six feet square. The living area, dining room, and kitchen are in one pyramid, and the bedrooms and baths in the other pyramid.

"I have reduced my sleeping time to about four to five hours regardless of physical activity," he wrote, and added, "But I always feel relaxed, confident, and good while in the house. I always wake up feeling good ... The dreams that I have are really vivid—or at least I can remember more, and they are more impressed upon me ... My feeling (physical) and my mental attitude in the morning are much more consistent than before sleeping in the pyramid (and they're very good)."

Mayfield continues: "I could go on forever. It has just been a beautiful experience."

Edwin and Marilyn Buxton and their family have lived in a pyramid house for about three years. Actually, their experiences with a pyramid home started in the summer of 1970 when they decided that their new home would be a pyramid. Buxton is a construction design engineer and has now established the Pyramid Design Division of E. D. Buxton & Associates, located at 520 Jackson Avenue in Charleston, Illinois. Due to the number of persons writing them for advice, they ask that those writing enclose a stamped self-addressed envelope. He and his wife designed their pyramid home and began construction in September 1973. They moved in on December 15, 1975.

The house is 56 feet 6 inches square and 37 feet in height—approximately the same as the Noble home. The first floor contains 2,704 square feet, the second floor 1,600 square feet, and the third floor 676 square feet. A basement contains an additional 2,296 square feet; a solarium contains 1,400 square feet, and a deck has 1,120 square feet. All in all, the total space is 9,796 square feet.

The first floor is used as the main living area, master bedroom, bath, utility and sewing room, kitchen with

Hallway connecting the two pyramids of twin-pyramid home.

Den area in twin-pyramid home.

indoor garden, dining room, living room, family room, and den. The second floor contains the children's suite, including three bedrooms, two playrooms, library, and bath. The third floor is an open room used for meditation and prayer and for treating various substances.

The basement is exposed on the east and south. It has two garages, two offices, two workshops, bath, pool equipment room, electrical room, mechanical and water treatment room. The solarium contains a pool, patio, and tropical tree garden. The 28 by 40 foot deck overlooks the valley from the solarium roof.

To satisfy the many inquiries which the Buxtons receive, they have drafted information sheets. They describe the pyramid and give their reasons for its design. As to special features, they state:

"1. Design was specifically planned for a pyramid, taking advantage of the unique possibilities. There is virtually no wasted space. All space enclosed by the pyramid is taken advantage of.

"2. Heating and cooling take advantage of temperature differences on each level and unique air flow pattern within the pyramid.

"3. The plan is designed to be an open, flowing plan with no hallways or dead areas.

"4. Windows are designed to take advantage of a wonderful view, solar angles for maximum heat in winter and shade in summer and sun entry into appropriate living areas at certain times of the day.

"5. Future plans include development of a solar system, and other features aimed at making this a self-sufficient home.

"6. Flexible areas are planned to be adaptable to future discoveries of the benefits of pyramid energy."

Pyramid home in southern Illinois owned by Ed and Marilyn Buxton. Area at lower left is to be glassed in to enclose garden and patio.

Marilyn Buxton has kept a diary of their pyramid experiences since moving into their home. Their story is a fascinating and provocative account. It is a personal story of people struggling to realize a dream, with all the frustrations and fulfillments usually accompanying such endeavors. More than this, it reflects the identity crises, the pain and joy experienced by people in the throes of transition in their lives. We could tell their story in abbreviated form, touching principally on the highlights, but it would not have the personal flavor, nor would the reader know the Buxtons as well, as having them tell their own story. In knowing the Buxtons one can better appreciate their experiences in their pyramid home. Following then, is their account of an adventure which

Southwest corner of Buxton home. Glass windows on south side face into living area. The open area below the concrete slab is to be glassed in for indoor garden.

started in the summer of 1970:

"'He did tell us this morning that this was going to happen. We should have been more careful.' I was brought out of my weary thoughts by Ed's comment, and had to think a moment before I realized what he meant. At 6 A.M. that morning we had been awakened by our three-year-old son, Dale, who was rather shaken by a nightmare—the first and only one he has ever had, to our knowledge. I recalled his excited recitation of his dream. 'A big black monster jumped at me and bited me!' I was stunned as I realized that both Dale this morning and Ed now were referring to the events which had just occurred.

"We spent the afternoon at Wyman Park in Sullivan, Illinois, the same place we always spend the first Sunday afternoon in June. It was June 6, 1976, the day of the forty-third annual Buxton Family Reunion. Afterward, as we followed Ed's cousin to see his new home, I recalled the first reunion I had attended nearly a dozen years ago. The discussion of the family tree and both glorious and notorious Buxtons of the past had been a new experience for me, the Cleveland-born and -bred granddaughter of an illiterate but wise Yugoslavian blacksmith immigrant. At our family gatherings it had often seemed to me as though the world had begun with my grandparents. I couldn't imagine any relatives before them. Yet this family knew of those members who had lived over two hundred years ago! The strength, independence, intelligence, and sometimes eccentricity which seemed to characterize this family could be seen in many of those fine rural people who were in attendance that day, including my husband.

"As we entered the yard, Allene, wife of the Buxton family historian, petted their large curly black dog as she told us about seeing him at the dog pound and feeling sorry enough for him to bring him home. A little later, about 6 P.M., as Dale was gently petting him we watched in horror as the black dog suddenly leaped at Dale, gripping Dale's right ear furiously with his teeth. When we freed him we saw a severely cut and torn ear, bleeding profusely on all sides with the lobe dangling precariously. The swollen, discolored ear, the pale, shaken child, and the agony he had endured during the medical treatment and stitching stayed in my mind as we drove home.

"Ed was right. The child had warned us exactly twelve hours earlier. I recalled Dale's comment after he had told us about the dream that morning. 'Don't worry, Mommy, I'll be all right. I smashed him so I'll be all right.'

"A precognitive dream! This was certainly more than we had bargained for. It had been six months since we moved into our rough, unfinished, mud-surrounded, leaky pyramid home. It had been more like moving in with a well-known familiar friend than moving into a cold, not yet personalized new house. We knew it well. We had conceived it, raised it from its infancy, dealt with it through the sunlight of its childhood and the windstorms of its youth, built it up, torn it down, and rebuilt it where necessary. Robin, Tammy, and Dale had played, eaten, and slept there while we worked. Dale had known it all of his life. It was like coming home finally. Just exactly six years ago, in June of 1970, while Ed was working on our house design, I was reading *Psychic Discoveries Behind the Iron Curtain*. My long interest in ancient Egypt and the pyramids as well as the new ideas presented by Ostrander and Schroeder prompted me to suggest to Ed that we adapt his basically square, pyramid-roofed house idea and actually build a scale model version of the Great Pyramid. Ed seemed to like the idea immediately, much to my surprise. In eight years of planning homes together, we had *never* found a single one we could agree on.

"We did some simple dehydration experiments and found that we could duplicate some of the results reported in the book. By using small cardboard models, we were able to dehydrate small amounts of liver and beef in hot, humid weather, without spoiling. Our controls outside the pyramid rotted, got maggots and bugs, and had to be thrown away. Meanwhile, we had done a considerable amount of thinking about the advantages of a pyramid-shaped house. The roof slope, nearly fifty-two degrees, is perfect for adaptation to solar energy, something my energy-conscious engineer husband was very interested in. Orienting the house to true north, facing the sides toward the four cardinal points, would also give us a true southern face for solar collectors. We thought of all the possibilities for storage, pull-outs, indoor gardens, closets, and bookshelves offered by the perimeter sloping area inside. Ed was intrigued with the engineering challenge and construction cost savings involved in building a house whose exterior was all roof and no walls! We like the simply pure geometric shape; basic, natural, and uncluttered, a statement against the angled, broken, disjointed, fragmented architectural style which seems to us to be representative of our disjointed, fragmented, cluttered society. Somehow, the pyramid just *felt* right for us, like the five acres we were looking at felt right. If it reduced the occurrence of colds and flu, preserved our meat, enhanced cosmic energies—well, that would be icing on the cake. It took us two more years before we had an agreeable floor plan, a good well, and enough money to begin construction. In September 1973, the pyramid building began. We moved in on December 15, 1975.

"In our first six months as pyramid dwellers several changes took place. I had begun to notice some mellowing changes taking place in Ed even before we moved, while he had been working on the pyramid. We had successfully repeated the dehydration experiments in our home. House plants which I had received when Dale was born suddenly took a new interest in life and outgrew their pots. New shoots and small two-inch or four-inch potted plants quickly made a large, green, healthy statement in behalf of the pyramid. I developed overnight the green thumb I had never had. Seeds I had started for my garden germinated in about one fourth the expected number of days.

"Robin, our eight-year-old daughter, had not added a

bit to her height in a year and a half. Now she had joined her younger sister Tammy and brother Dale by growing nearly two and one half inches in the first five months in our home. Several of us had heard on occasion unexplained distant 'voices' which resembled the sound of a radio playing just out of earshot. But, most noticeable of all, no one had been really sick with flu or colds or virus infections since we had moved. Due to our severe respiratory allergies, sinus infections, sore throats, and earaches had been a constant presence. *None at all* for six months seemed to us to be a miracle. With dowsing wires we had detected energy currents throughout the house, not just at the King's Chamber level. We were suspicious of the energy being very weak along the east side of the house, much stronger on the west because of our consistently poor results on tomatoes, liver, and plants placed there.

"We loved the house, sawdust, nails, unfinished roof and all. We found that the heating and cooling system which Ed had planned worked wonderfully to keep us toasty warm and fairly efficiently considering the condition of the house. The scenery was magnificent through winter's ice, spring's greening, and summer's fullness. At times we sensed a deep feeling of relaxation and peace. We had gotten more than we bargained for!

"On the other hand there were those things which we would never have wanted to bargain for, like mud. Not just surrounding the exterior of the house, but usually brought in to dry on the floor and furniture by any family member or visitor who entered. The roof sealer which we had used between the asbestos board panels, the same stuff that carried a twenty-year guarantee against drying, cracking, or peeling, had nevertheless dried, cracked, and peeled. The rain was coming in by the bucketsful. We weren't interested in shingles or lapped siding and the tremendous exposure to the sun with alternating expansion and contraction on the pyramid's faces eliminated most of the roof coverings we considered as replacements for the errant sealer. Then there were the insects. By this time pyramid books and articles had appeared and we read several accounts of insects being repelled or killed by pyramids. We waged a constant war on flies, spiders, mosquitoes, wasps, ants, two breeds of cockroaches, and several other unfamiliar and more exotic creatures. They had lived here in the woods in peace and obviously had no intention of turning the pyramid over to us without a battle. Strangely enough, they were never found on the west side of the house on any floor.

"The first few weeks after we moved in, Ed and I had severe headaches and all of us had experienced mild nausea and diarrhea at times. And visitors—did we have visitors! There were those who left with the children's portable television, those who broke out the basement window to enter and have a beer party, those who damaged the garage overhead door while forcing it open, those who damaged the lock on the kitchen door, those who took all the small power tools, those who backed into my car in the driveway, and of course, those who walked in without asking while we were home and took photos!

"And the back-breaking labor. Ed's weariness and struggle in trying to build a structure this size cannot be described. While he had some help the first summer in framing the structure, he now usually worked alone as carpenter, plumber, electrician, concrete former, roofer, and chief maintenance man. I often suffered great pangs of self-pity as I removed splinters, salved blisters, and rubbed sore aching muscles. Though always active, ambitious, and alert, nothing in my experience or college work had completely prepared me for hauling lumber, scaffolding, concrete forms, cases of nails, and cement blocks, nor for shoveling mud out, sand in, rocks out, mud in, sand out, rocks in. It seemed endless. All this after working at our regular jobs. Our family and friends commented frequently on how much we were probably enjoying doing it ourselves and how nice it was that we were working on this together. Ed and I knew we had long ago passed the point where the work was enjoyable. We quarreled and disagreed about everything and the many differences between us at times loomed unmanageably as we tried to build a home uniquely planned for us, our life-style, our tastes. *Whose* life-style and tastes? We were so opposite! We suffered depression, nervousness, and irritability. We saw jealousy, anger, fears, insecurities, and other carefully repressed feelings surfacing. Our spats were becoming less frequent now and we had some good times of warmth and companionship between them. Yet I kept wondering about the constant peace, tranquillity, increased vitality, loving kindness, and spiritual growth that pyramid users were reporting now with increasing zeal.

"Dale's weak but continuous pleas of 'Take me to my home, Mommy' were finally answered as we drove around the concrete forms which would one day be a retaining wall. He went to bed without any medication for pain, slept soundly, and never again had a moment of discomfort with his ear. By the following weekend, it was completely healed, with only a slight scar line on the lobe. That weekend, Ed and I attended Christian Marriage Encounter in St. Louis, a weekend of work on communication training for married couples. During the weekend we experienced a spiritual miracle of love. Now as I look back to that time, just a year ago, I see that June of 1976 marked a new life, a new beginning. Rebirth always involves learning, growing, changing, and some discomfort and pain. The first year of nearly daily exposure to our pyramid, June 1975 to June 1976, seems to have been a time of purging—clearing cobwebs of habits, pulling out the weeds of repressions, and generally preparing us for what was to come.

"On July 5, 1976, I awoke, glowing, excited, and somewhat mystified. I had experienced a dream of such clarity and vividness that it must be called a vision. It involved religious symbolism that included both John the

Baptist and Christ in direct communication with me. This was most unusual, since my religious beliefs have always been far from traditional. The dream focused upon using pyramid-treated water for healing children and I was clearly admonished to never forget that the ultimate source of this healing power came through me and the water from the one source of all power, the creative, loving intelligence of God. We have treated water in several locations in our pyramid without being able to detect any changes in it, nor have we discovered any healing effects from its use yet.

"Later in July, our wonderful trip to Fort Collins, Colorado, for a solar energy conference at Colorado State and our return to California and Arizona reminded us of the variety of nature's creative beauty in contrast to the sameness of man's dull efforts to build.

"Several times in the last year we have experienced moments when the energy in our third-floor room was high enough to cause immediate physical sensations similar to those caused by exposure to a low-voltage electrical current. Many visitors here have experienced it also. At times it cannot be felt at all, at others it is so strong that I cannot remain in the room for very long without feeling uncomfortable. I feel it as a tingling feeling throughout my body, a slight ringing in my ears, and an uncomfortable feeling in the area of the solar plexus. We have seen hair stand out on people's arms and on two occasions, the energy in one spot has been strong enough to cause dizziness and nearly unconsciousness. It affects some people with greater strength than others. Many visitors who were totally unaware of our experiences have had very strong reactions.

"The growth of house plants has been quite spectacular. The speed of growth is especially noticeable in cactus plants. We preserved fresh, fully ripened tomatoes for a month without any decay last summer. We have dehydrated ground beef, beef liver, fresh eggs, bananas, and several other items without any evidence of spoiling.

Growth in both the children and plants seems to have reached an optimum level and normalized. We have been free of colds and flu for nearly two years. We are very hesitant to attribute these effects to pyramid energy. Our lives and our environment have changed. All we can say is that these things have happened.

"We continue our work and have given increasing attention to food production in planning indoor garden areas as well as preservation of our summer outdoor garden produce. Ed's plans include the design of a solar system to supplement our heat pump as well as a geothermal design aimed at eventually providing for all of our heat and electricity. We continue to develop new skills and revive old ones. Our goal is to be able to have a self-contained environment as much as possible. We want alternatives to energy controllers and freedom from food additives. We educate our children at home, using school as a supplement, and make our own clothes. We are active participants in local community affairs, yet we want to be as prepared as possible for independence, if the need arises. Although we still have setbacks, our peace and unity as a family are growing. Our good health continues. Our future looks exciting, though unknown. We have begun studying the Bible and are amazed at its clarity and relevance. Whatever forces are at work here seem to be working for our benefit.

"'And we know that all things work together for good to them that love God, to them who are the called according to his purpose.' Romans 8:28."

The common experiences of the Nobles, the Buxtons, Mayfield, and Benini unfold in somewhat dramatic fashion. Perhaps the most significant commonly shared experience is the spiritual growth attending living inside a pyramid. Each has kept his or her separate diary or log, uninfluenced by other pyramid dwellers. Yet the spiritual awakening was identified by each as the most important development—sufficient, it would appear, to change their lives. It is interesting to note that visitors to the pyramid homes also noted an atmosphere of spirituality. Such testimonials should put those at ease who have questioned whether the forces of the pyramid are beneficial to man. Once in a great while we receive such an inquiry.

Other commonalities include—with those who have children—initially, sudden spurts of growth, reaching, they say, an optimum level and then normal, continued growth; outstanding plant growth rates; health and a decrease in illness; restful sleep—sometimes less than before—and vivid, meaningful dreams; food tastes better and generally is more easily preserved; mental alertness and positive outlook on life, along with enhanced creativity. Differences appear to be minor and where these occur they may be due to interior construction and design of the pyramids, differences in materials, etc. Of course, different results in some of the experiments, such as the treatment of water, were noted when sunspot activity was either high or low.

Earlier we described our experiments with pyramids with indented sides and discussed findings which might indicate that pyramids so constructed would produce better results than those with flat sides. Due to the extent and variety of planes—walls, ceilings, furniture, appliances, etc.—inside of pyramid homes which would divert and alter the paths of energy fields, it might be preferable to have unindented exteriors on pyramid homes. In view of the factors outlined, we leave this matter to the discretion of the reader. Another point to consider is that homes constructed with indented exteriors might have noticeable locations of intense energy. The Buxtons found this to be the case in a spot located on the stairs near the third floor. Judging from our experiments with laser beams, this is where we would expect to find an unusual energy field. The tachyon energy field entering through the west side of the roof at the apex would be reflected essentially downward and create an interference pattern. If the force field at this location is found to be too intense, the area could be covered with sheet rock or other material to form a ceiling over the area. We might speculate that in the near future it will be possible to determine the exact locations for interior walls for optimum results by means of the laser or computer.

It is worthwhile to discover in view of rising fuel costs that the large homes of the Nobles and the Buxtons, involving several thousand cubic feet of space, have heating costs less than those for conventional homes. Gary and Debbie Noble's home is electrically heated and yet costs very little more to heat than nearby homes only a fraction of the size. Despite the Illinois winters the Buxtons were amazed that their heating costs were running only about $400 to $450 per year at current rates. This is most likely due to the reasons explained earlier by Buxton. Also, heat rises, and since the pyramid provides a steep slope to the apex there is less space overhead for heat loss.

In answer to our questions, the Buxtons provided us the following information. Although we have included their story, the following provides additional information and insights into their experiences:

"1. We noticed a sudden growth spurt in all three children after moving into the house. This same growth spurt seems to take place in plants. However, it seems to have reached an optimum level and then further growth seems much more normal in speed. The big difference is that the children and the plants are so hale and hearty! One lady wrote asking if our kids were giants or extremely tall—like seven or eight feet...I can assure you, however, that our children are quite average in height and weight, including our four-year-old, who has spent nearly his whole life under the influence of this pyramid. My plants are fantastic. The most dramatic effect can be seen in my cactus plants, which have grown unbelievably. The kids have always been good students.

"2. There has been a *dramatic* change in our health. Our entire family have been lifelong allergy sufferers. We are still allergic. However, the annual two or three flu bouts and constant colds have disappeared. Never before in all my thirty-six years have I gone a year without a cold. I have not had one in two years now. Also, none of our children ever made it through a winter without several colds. Two of the kids got a mild cold last October. We removed their bedroom window and covered the hole with canvas. That night it got very cold and *rained* into their room. They were well in a few days, however. No one in the family has had flu since we moved in. There are other factors which may have contributed to this.

"3. We have not noticed any change in foods we use. However, we have no evidence of pyramid energy in our kitchen. This may be due to the metal and electricity in our appliances or to the *low energy* we seem to have in the northeast corner of our home. (I know this is exactly the opposite of what you seem to have found.) We have carried out many food dehydration experiments on liver, ground beef, egg, etc. Things seem to dehydrate quite nicely *if left uncovered.* Foods covered with plastic wrap to keep out air have spoiled, however. We suspect the unique air current in the pyramid may contribute to the dehydration. I have also preserved marigolds and kept ripe tomatoes for nearly a month without spoiling.

"4. We usually sleep six to seven hours a night, which was our previous schedule. We do sleep better and more soundly. We also are extremely active and are involved in a great many community and professional activities besides building our house. We are still tired a lot, but probably because we don't ever seem to stop working until we have used all our energy. The big difference, though, is the dramatic reduction in illness in spite of our work and weariness. Our resistance to infection is strong.

"5. Our son had a precognitive dream last summer, June 6, 1976, and on July 5, I had a dream which was so unusual and vivid that I must call it a vision. We also believe we have grown considerably in our interpersonal relationships as a family. In our third-floor room, there have been several occasions when visitors who were not aware of pyramid energy felt a kind of current. Most describe it as feeling like electricity. I have experienced it on several occasions but cannot seem to relate it to anything specific. Most of the time the energy seems to be present on clear sunny days or the evenings following them! Just when I begin to think there is nothing to the pyramid energy business, that everything can be explained in some other way, we seem to have a strong physical feeling—almost like a sign."

Most recently the Buxtons wrote us:

"I think you can tell that all four corners of the pyramid are maintained on the structure. However, for about the last two months, the baseline on the south has not been intact (temporarily) due to some work we were doing where it meets the deck. Interestingly, my plants, which are primarily along the windows on the south side, have been doing poorly after two years of thriving. They are turning brown, scrawny, and have slowed in growth. I believe they will recover when we get the south baseline fixed. The solarium on the south will be completely underground except for the south side. The large opening in the picture will be sloping windows. The deck connects to a concrete walk which goes around all four sides of the house. The walk meets the base of the pyramid all around the perimeter.

"We have had many visitors who were concerned about effects on our children. I can say without hesitation that *our* pyramid home has done them absolutely no harm that we can detect. They are happy, healthy, friendly, successful in school, and active in school and community. Due to the need for a required physical, I saw our family doctor yesterday. He commented on the pronounced and unexplained improvement in the health of all five of us in the last two years.

"We have made some exterior changes on the east and will begin some experiments to check results. We hope we corrected energy in the northeast corner where the

kitchen and utility room are located. Due to the extremely
rapid spoiling of tomatoes and vegetables kept there, no
growth in any of the plants I've tried there, meat samples
which rotted there instead of dehydrating, and other
informal observations, I had decided not to put my pantry
there. We had decided to move it to the dining room area.
We also have put closet and toy storage in that area on the
second floor and moved our little boy's bedroom to the
west side. Incidentally, you may notice on our drawing
that all our beds are aligned to the north. The master
bedroom and our boy's bedroom are located between the
corners on a diagonal across the pyramid due to energy.
We plan to shift the girls' beds south and put desk areas in
the north corners of their rooms.

"We have had a spiritual awakening and development
since we have been living here. We have felt the presence
of God very clearly several times and believe He is
working in our lives. We have grown from a rather robot-
like, liberal, Sunday-only, symbolically interpreted view
of the Bible and church to an alive, active, literal belief
which seems to fit with our learning and philosophies. All
of the threads of our life and experience seem to be
unifying around the core truths of all religious beliefs.
Our private Bible studying during the last year and a half
has been a potent force for change in our lives. Much of
this has developed from my dreams and a series of
amazing 'coincidences.' We believe that God is the source
of all power and energy and we have the freedom to use
the forces He makes available to us for good or evil,
toward growth or disintegration. Thus we shy away from
self-aggrandizing experiential phenomena or 'thrills.' I
especially feel a closeness with the Edgar Cayce philosophy.

"We have found that many of our visitors who come
from out of state are also Christians—both Catholic and
Protestant. Many are well educated, well read, widely
traveled, and fairly 'successful' people. Several times we
have discussed ways in which we see pyramid discoveries

setting the first planks in the bridge which will eventually connect science and religion so that each proves the truth of the other. Although we are active members of the First Christian Church, Disciples of Christ, I consider myself to be non-denominational. I believe the truth and heart of all major religions is basically the same.

"It is hard for me to explain this—while several of our informal experiments have made other people take note of pyramid energy, what has been the most convincing to me has been the subjective but very clear physical and spiritual experiences that have happened to me but cannot be proven to anyone else. We have also come to believe that God has been guiding us throughout this project. We don't know why yet, but expect we will find out when He wants us to! We have done most of our planning through intuition and inspiration and thought of the sound reasons and explanations *after* the fact. We are trying to learn to be more and more open to the influence of the one Almighty Creative Spirit which we believe is guiding us. I must point out, I did *not* talk or think this way three years ago. Though always somewhat intuitive, logic and reason were our most dominant mode. We never cease to be amazed that some of the best features of our house have actually been accidents! 'Divine guidance'?"

NINE

Confounding Newton

The Riddle of the Gyroscope

A NEW Age, a rapidly changing world with the prospect of awesome tomorrows—both beautiful and frightening—these speculations claim a growing portion of our conversations and communications these days. Science, technology, space travel, inner space, instant computerized knowledge, these breathtaking developments have brought us to a certain awareness that we are perched on the threshold of a world whose realities are no more permanent than the images cast by a kaleidoscope.

It is difficult to write any scientific treatise today with sufficient speed to prevent its obsolescence by the time it reaches print. Research in this solid-state, computerized age moves that rapidly. One cannot linger long over the test tubes and drawing board without discovering the dust of his peers settling on his findings. One works long hours, drinks a lot of coffee, ignores those activities in the world not having an immediate and visible application to the task at hand, and hopes that that world is still there when he has a chance to peek out the window. You add up your data, check your findings, number the pages, and stake your claim. One doesn't imagine for a moment that the job is done, that any kind of final word has been written or conclusion drawn. This simply doesn't happen in today's hyperventilating world.

Faced with what would need be the ending chapter to this book, we found ourselves struggling with frustrations. On the one hand, we felt satisfied that exciting and new information was presented in the completed chapters. But on the other hand, there was the concern that important research remained to be done. Along with this predicament, however, was the haunting awareness that this would always be so. Whether this is always true of research, we do not know, but non-closure is something one has to live with when investigating pyramid phenomena. The case is not in on what pyramids are all about, how and why they work, and the implications of the discoveries already made. Nor do we know who were the builders of the great parent pyramid and what they had in mind. But our respect for them continues to grow.

The information contained in this chapter was held to the last in order to conduct as many experiments in this particular field as possible. But while the experiments will continue, we reached a sufficient plateau of exploration that we can pass along some worthwhile and provocative observations. We would counsel the reader here that what we offer on the preceding pages and the pages to follow should not be construed as definitive studies. The scientific community has a habit of requiring experiments to be repeated many, many times before findings are offered as conclusive. It's not a bad habit; this insistence on precision and repeatability has done well in pushing aside veils of our environment and ourselves. It is difficult to argue with success. Yet there is another approach to the philosophers' stone which has its merits. Preliminary experiments and observations—represented as such and nothing more—are necessary in order to initiate serious research. These are the seeds of research.

What excited us during the early stages of writing this book were our discoveries of unusual weight loss of solids inside pyramids and the erratic behavior of spinning gyroscopes. Aware of the possible implications of these findings, we delayed describing them until we could develop additional research tools and more reliable measurements.

Our earlier suspicion that pyramid results were linked to sunspot acitivity now appears to be supported by our observations and those of others. As mentioned earlier, sunspots are believed to be caused by large magnetic fields—some of them thousands of miles in diameter—on the surface of the sun. These fields reach the earth via the solar wind. Rich in electromagnetic energy and, according to our theory, possibly tachyons, these fields profoundly affect life processes on this planet. They also have a great deal to do with weather conditions, according to a growing number of scientists. For example, widespread droughts apparently occur during times of low sunspot acitivty.

By correlating dates when pyramids produce maximum and minimum effects with U.S. Government sunspot charts, we learned that the periods when the pyramids produced the greatest results—plant growth rates and movement, dehydration, desirable changes in milk, meditation, etc.—coincided with times of high sunspot activity. When very little appeared to be happening to objects and subjects exposed to pyramid space, it was discovered that sunspot activity was at the low swing of the cycle.

What are the implications of these findings? For one thing, it appears evident that the pyramid serves as a sensitive barometer of energy fields in our environment. Pyramid activity does not entirely cease during times of low sunspot periods and it may be that pyramids can make available to us additional energy sources than are normally accessible to us during these times. A question we might ask is whether the builders of the Great Pyramid were aware of sunspot cycles and whether this was one of the reasons for the construction. But like the other questions having to do with ancient knowledge and intent, one can only speculate.

Questions of this nature continually haunt us, but never more so than recently when we discovered a curious fact about the locations of the various pyramids of the world.

We were studying isomagnetic charts of the earth. It is believed that when the Great Pyramid was constructed, the magnetic field on the plain of Giza was at zero declination. (The compass needle pointed to magnetic north.)

To explain the word "declination" we quote from a United States Coast and Geodetic Survey booklet, *The Magnetism of the Earth*—Publication 40-1, 1962. It states, in part: "There is a widespread belief that the compass points toward the magnetic pole. As a matter of fact, in large areas the magnetic north differs 10° or more from the direction of the magnetic pole."

The earth's lines of magnetic force are constantly changing. These changes are known as secular changes. In some portions of the earth the secular change will be extremely small over long periods of time and then, for unknown reasons, will begin to vary. Because of this, it can be assumed that over the centuries the Great Pyramid has not always been at zero declination.

Yet the latest isomagnetic charts we have reveal the fascinating fact that the Great Pyramid once again stands at zero declination!

Intrigued by this fact, we marked the location of other known pyramid structures of the world on the chart. We

Simplified isogonic chart of the world (courtesy of the U.S. Navy Hydrographic Office and the National Oceanic and Atmospheric Administration). The numbers correspond to locations of the following various known pyramids: 1— Shensi pyramids in China. 2—The great white Himalayan pyramid. 3—Angkor pyramid. 4—Central Siberian pyramid. 5—King's Templar pyramid. 6—Pyramid mound at Collinsville, Illinois. 7—Reported underwater pyramid in Bermuda Triangle. 8—Mayan pyramids. 9—Egyptian pyramids.

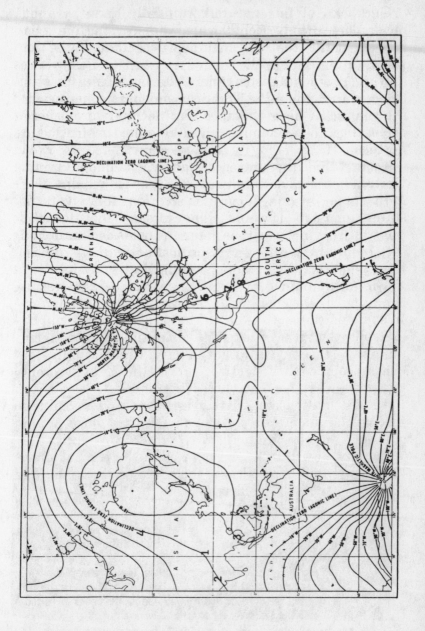

could scarcely believe what we saw...These pyramids were, each and every one, located very near the line of zero declination! This was the case even though the zero declination line for the earth's isomagnetic field weaves up and down and varies widely from latitudinal lines as it circumvents the earth. This discovery immediately raised the question as to whether zero declination existed at these locations when the pyramids were constructed. As it seems too remote to be mere coincidence, we would assume that the ancients had ways of determining magnetic fields and that zero declination was one of the criteria for selecting a pyramid site. Were they aware that isomagnetic fields would change and that these locations would from time to time return to zero declination? Is there anything different or critical about these periods? Does the fact that the world's pyramids are now located at zero declination have any significance? Interesting

Nine-and-a-half-pound weight inside sixteen-foot pyramid. Experiment demonstrates loss of weight in pyramid.

questions, perhaps, but for the moment the answers go begging.

While we cannot find our way back to the intentions and motivations of ancient engineers, we can pursue the behavior of pyramids in our world today. Research with cardboard, wood, plastic, and glass pyramids provides sufficiently exciting, and sometimes surprising, results to satisfy the most curious. Fascinated with our theory of tachyons and their relationship to pyramids, we devised an experiment to measure the presence of these faster-than-light particles within pyramid enclosures. As the theoretical tachyon is a negative form of energy, we reasoned that an increase in tachyon energy could possibly result in weight change for an object placed inside.

We constructed a balance on a fulcrum in a manner that one arm of the balance was outside and the other arm inside a sixteen-foot pyramid. Metal objects of identical weights of nine and a half pounds were placed on each arm and perfectly balanced. Twenty-four hours later the weight inside the pyramid was found to have lost one and a half ounces.

Additional tests continued to produce the weight-loss phenomenon. Further measurements were conducted by using a scale that is sensitive to one tenth of a grain (there are 437.6 grains per ounce). Objects were weighed and then placed inside a twenty-inch glass pyramid with indented sides and solid capstone. All objects were placed in the King's Chamber area. Iron weighing 1,094 grains lost 3.3 grains in two hours, 5.1 grains in eleven hours. Soft aluminum weighing 1,004 grains lost 5.2 grains in one hour, but aluminum alloy weighing 755 grains neither lost nor gained weight in twelve hours. Soft copper weighing 795.6 grains lost 4.9 grains in one hour, and 5.2 grains in fourteen hours.

In another experiment, a ten-pound block of iron, ten pounds of sugar sealed in plastic bags, and a sixty-four-ounce piece of solid plastic were placed inside the sixteen-foot pyramid on October 22, 1977. When weighed on November 12, 1977, it was found that the iron had lost sixty-one grams, the sugar had lost fifty grams, and the plastic fifty-two grams. The plastic lost a higher percentage of weight than the iron or sugar.

The balancing device was used for another experiment. An iron weight of nine and a half pounds was hung on the interior end of the balance. This was counterbalanced on the outer end with a plastic bucket holding onyx gravel. The bucket was then covered with aluminum foil and taped in place to prevent condensation of moisture on the pebbles. Beneath this weight on the inside of the pyramid a fixed weight of ten and half pounds was solidly fixed. The idea was to see if the spacing between the two masses would be altered by some force inside the pyramid. According to our model, this force would be tachyon flow. The spacing between the two masses was measured at one eighth inch.

The following morning Pettit discovered that the weights were more than one half inch apart. Previous to leaving for the night, Pettit had measured not only the distance between the ground weight and the bottom on the outside of the pyramid but also the distance from the bottom of the pyramid to the suspended weight on the inside. Apparently a repulsion existed between the two masses. It was necessary to add twenty-two grams of weight to the upper weight to bring the balance into the position it had originally occupied.

The lower, fixed weight was removed in order to see if the upper weight would return to its original position. However, this did not happen and it appeared that the mass of the iron weight had in some manner been reduced. Two days later the position of the weight was checked again but it had not moved.

Another balance was constructed. This balance was sensitive to within two grams. It was a short balance and consisted of a rigid pipe with a knife-edge fulcrum. Brackets were attached on each end of the balance. A ten-

A plastic ball experiment used to measure power source within a pyramid.

pound bag of sugar was opened and placed upon two plastic bags. Sugar was removed until the weight was exactly ten pounds. The sugar was then double-sealed inside the two plastic bags and placed in the King's Chamber area upon a suspended five by ten inch solid copper plate.

The following morning the sugar was weighed and found to have lost twenty-seven grams in weight (approximately one ounce).

The sugar was placed a second time inside the pyramid

but this time with a slanting gable roof covering it. As our experiments with the laser beam indicated that the gable roof altered the vertical deflection of the light within the King's Chamber, we wondered if this arrangement would change the accumulation of tachyons in the sugar granules. The next morning the sugar was weighed and this time it was found that it had lost fifty-one grams of weight ... almost doubling the weight loss in the previous experiment!

Did the sugar granules actually lose some of their mass, or had some moisture been removed by pyramid force? One would assume that the sealed plastic sacks would prevent a loss of moisture, but then an unbroken hen's egg is dehydrated inside a pyramid.

Cavendish balances have been used since the 1700s to demonstrate the attraction of one mass for another. If the experimenter finds that there is some combination of materials that will cause one mass to have a greater or lesser attraction for the other mass, this demonstrates a power potential.

The Cavendish balance seemed to be an excellent device to measure a power source within the pyramid. The balance was constructed by fixing two five-inch balls at each end of a rigid wooden bar. The balls were made of poured plastic into which stainless steel bolts had been imbedded. The bar was mounted on a fixed base. A second bar of rigid aluminum was used on which four-inch balls were mounted. The balls were made by pouring plastic into glass Christmas bulbs. To the center of the bar was tied four-pound-test nylon monofilament fishing line. A twenty-nine-inch pyramid was used in the experiment and the four-and-a-half-inch capstone was made of cast plastic, an organic material. A vertical hole was drilled through the capstone and the nylon line was threaded through the hole in order that the aluminum bar with its plastic balls could be suspended in the pyramid directly above the other fixed bar sitting on its base. The nylon line was tied to a rigid support above the pyramid.

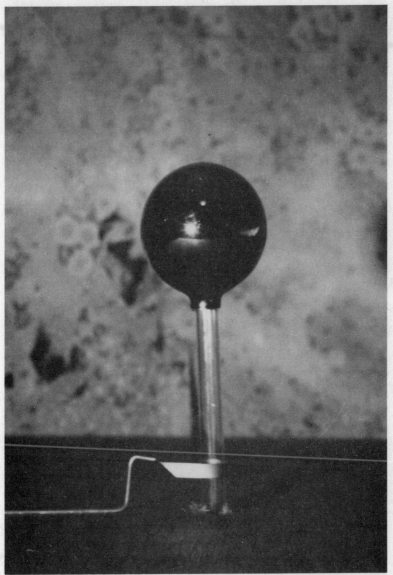

Close-up of plastic ball used inside pyramid to measure
power source.

Prior to using the nylon line in the experiment a weight was suspended from it for two days so that any twist could be corrected and any stretching would have already taken place.

The suspended bar was hung directly over the fixed bar. Rather than put any twist in the line, since all twist had been removed and the suspended bar did not move, the lower bar was adjusted so that the balls were within one quarter inch of the other balls. Any movement of attraction or repulsion would be noted by means of a mirror attached to the suspended nylon line. The laser beam was directed to the mirror and reflected to a chart sixteen feet distant. Thus any movement would be noted by the mirror reflecting light to a scale.

No change was noted during the first hour. The following morning, however, it was found that the balls had moved apart five inches, the maximum distance they could move before they rested against the sides of the pyramid.

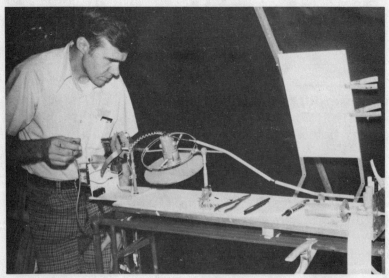

Edmund Pettit, Ed Pettit's son, operates gyroscope test unit inside pyramid.

The balls were again moved to a close proximity but again began to move apart. Being unable to keep the balls together, the hook holding the line was twisted two turns counterclockwise. This brought the balls together but once again they started moving apart. The suspended balls continued to move until they rested against the sides of the pyramid. Finally, eleven turns were taken in the line and there was a visible twist in the filament but the separation still persisted.

We are at a loss to explain this phenomenon. The distance is too great for like static charges to be involved and the balls are too heavy to account for such movement. The impression is that the balls are repelling each other, but to repel such masses over a distance of five inches would require a very large magnetic field. Since the masses are of plastic inside glass balls and supported by an aluminum rod, magnetism can be discounted.

The Cavendish balance was removed from the pyramid and during a period of two days the repulsion between the balls gradually diminished. Four days later the balls remained stationary, regardless of the proximity to one another.

When one considers that the balls repulsed each other for a distance of more than five inches and against the twist in the line, it can be seen that this is an unusual set of circumstances. Can the movement be explained by the concentration of tachyons creating a negative space-time energy field?

After the experiences with the weights and the apparent changes in the mass in and out of the pyramid, we began to speculate as to the nature of centrifugal and centripetal forces in the pyramid. A gyroscope seemed to be the logical device to test these forces.

With a gyroscope, the spinning wheel resists a movement along the axis of the wheel. It tends to twist to one side or another according to the direction of the rotation. We assumed that if there was some change in the apparent mass of the wheel in the pyramid it would

Edmund Pettit adjusting gyroscope test unit outside pyramid.

tend to have either a more pronounced twisting or a decrease in twisting depending upon the action of the tachyons as they are attracted to the mass of the rotating wheel.

We reasoned that a gyroscopic test would be invaluable

both from the standpoint of any differences that might be noticed in the force needed to move the axis (or axle) of the gyroscope against the gyroscopic action, as well as for the exact measurements of the movement of the rotor. We reasoned that the rotor would need more force to move the axle in a lateral line when the gyroscope was outside the pyramid than when the unit was inside an indented pyramid.

Pettit constructed a gyroscope by using a small fractional horsepower shunt-wound twenty-seven-volt aircraft motor turning at 5,600 RPM. A three-inch, half-inch-thick, steel flywheel was used. The motor was suspended three quarters of an inch from the flywheel by means of four springs attached to the motor flange and supported by vertical supports. The motor was hung so that the flywheel was at the bottom and most of the motor was above the springs.

When the motor was revved up and the top of the motor was moved horizontally away from the operator, the motor above the springs tended to swing to the left. This was caused by the flywheel tending to twist the unit from the gyroscopic effect. The unit was tilted a predetermined amount by an automatic gear motor unit which tilted the motor and rotor nearly one hundred and eighty degrees so that the unit was nearly upended, at which time the unit was released automatically and allowed to return by gravity into its original position.

As the rotor or spinning wheel was suspended on springs, the attached motor exerted a twist upon the support springs as an attempt was made to turn the motor and rotor in a straight line. At the start the motor and rotor were vertical to the earth, but when the activating motor moved the unit from the vertical up to and through the horizontal, the rotor exerted a twisting effect on the springs. The twisting effect was transferred to a flexible cable which was in turn connected to a horizontally sliding member holding a marking pen in the vertical position.

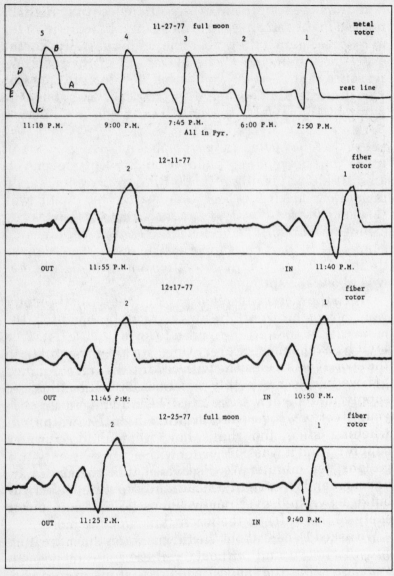

Four traces from gyroscopic test unit.

As the motor and rotor twisted on the springs, the cable was pulled or pushed, resulting in the pen being moved in direct proportion to the amount of movement of the rotor. The pen then made a continuous line on a moving strip of paper which was being pulled by a gear motor at right angles to the pen. The paper strip moved at a steady rate of one inch for each six seconds, or ten inches per minute.

On each strip (see charts) can be seen two straight horizontal lines, lighter than the center line. The thinner lines are guidelines so that amplitude of movement can be more readily discerned. The heavier line from the right side begins as a straight and horizontal line; this is the line scribed when the gyroscope rotor was running but the unit as a whole was stationary. Each strip should be read from right to left.

With the rotor rotating the strip motor was started and the paper began to move. The automatic gear motor turned the gyroscopic unit until it was nearly upended, nearly one hundred and eighty degrees, at which point the unit was automatically released.

Four charts are shown. The top one is with a metal rotor, while the balance are with organic (Masonite) rotors.

The top chart, 11-27-77 (full moon), shows the rest line moving upward as the gear motor upended the unit, resulting in a twisting motion and subsequent movement of the scribed line. The balance of the tests can be traced in a similar manner.

The marking pen traced the twist of the rotor as it was moved through the changes in the patterns as the unit was released and dropped to its original position.

As the rotor created a twisting motion against the supporting springs, the motion was transferred to the moving tape. Any change in apparent mass could then be determined.

The third chart reveals no changes from outside to inside the pyramid. The bottom chart shows a lesser amplitude of twist inside the pyramid than outside. The

Tape feed for gyroscope test unit with markers in place.

top chart, dated 11-27-77, reveals an increase of amplitude from test No. 1, taken at 2:50 P.M. inside the pyramid. It was a time of the full moon. Tests Nos. 2, 3, and 4 were run during the day; the last test, No. 5, was run at 11:10 P.M., at which time the maximum amplitude was noted. Test No. 5 is lettered. As the base line extends over from test No. 4 it can be seen that there is a sudden rise in the line (A) which was caused by the twist of the rotor as the motor was lifted from the vertical to a nearly upended position by the gear motor. The motor was released at this point and the motor and rotor began the descent toward normal rest position by gravity. The line drops nearly vertically to point (C), well past rest position, then rises to point (D), then settles to rest position (E).

It is interesting to note that in test No. 1 the rise to (B) is comparatively slight, and the return to (C) is nearly corresponding to the balance of the other four tests. Also note the differences in the rebound to (D). The rebound is accented as the tests progress.

The metal rotor was left on the unit from 2:50 P.M. past 11:10 P.M., when the final test was run. We did not consider that the continued exposure to the concentrated tachyons might alter subsequent tests, but this appears to be the case.

We envisioned that the accumulation of negative energy would cause—if any change was noted—a decrease in amplitude as the tests progressed, rather than the results actually noted. A heavier rotor results in increased twist being noted as the axis is turned on such a unit.

It appeared that with increased time exposure to the pyramid shape and with rapid rotation, the rotor increased in mass as the tests continued. This would not happen, as we saw it, if the rotor actually accumulated negative energy. Instead this would have resulted in a lesser amplitude of the scribed lines. Evidently, the change in the rotor was somewhat permanent, for tests run over the next six weeks continued to produce the same pattern as noted in test No. 5, the final test in the series described.

It would seem that inasmuch as we had an apparent decrease in the ten-pound metal mass which was suspended in a stationary manner inside the pyramid, and since we had an apparent increase in mass of a rotating mass, we must assume that the moving mass has strange characteristics indeed. Does the rapid motion of the atoms at or near the rim of the rotor result in an alteration of the tachyon force?

The next four strip charts were made with an organic fiber rotor, made of tempered hardboard. In the second chart it appears that there was a slight increase in mass during test No. 2 over No. 1. No. 3 chart shows no apparent change while test No. 4 shows a definite increase in apparent mass. Also note the increase in the changes of the scribed line as the rotor returned to rest position.

We have detected no change in the rotors after exposure as regards weight. We have speculated that perhaps the tachyon energy as it is absorbed into a moving disc reacts differently than it does as it is absorbed into one at rest. If we envision, for example, one molecule or atom at the rim of the rotor when traveling at a high rate of speed, it will move from one point in time to another point in time. When we take all the atoms on the rim into consideration, we may find that tachyons are attracted to the concentration of apparent mass and thereby more energy is absorbed by the rotor than if the mass was at rest.

A number of years ago a group of Russian scientists, headed by N. S. Kozyrev, conducted extensive exploration into the enigma of time. They termed their study "The Possibility of Experimental Study of the Properties of Time." The basis for their study was that cause and effect are always separated by space, therefore between them there also exists a small time difference. They explained that there is a time interval between even the slightest change in matter. The electron circling the atomic nucleus will move from one point in its orbit to another, but no matter how close the points are, there is still a difference in time, however small.

The Russians wanted to determine what role time played in matter. The question asked was whether matter changes as it passes from one point to another point in time, and what the differences would be. They built elaborate test equipment and conducted exhaustive tests using a gyroscopic wheel. They reasoned that the matter at the surface of a rapidly rotating wheel would pass one point in time, continuously, to another point in time, giving them predetermined velocity and passage of time.

The scientists established that when the rotor was rotating clockwise it gained eight milligrams in weight, and when the rotor was rotating counterclockwise it lost four milligrams in weight. The rotor was small. It measured only 1.77 inches in diameter and weighed slightly more than one fifth of an ounce, so the change in weight was comparatively large.

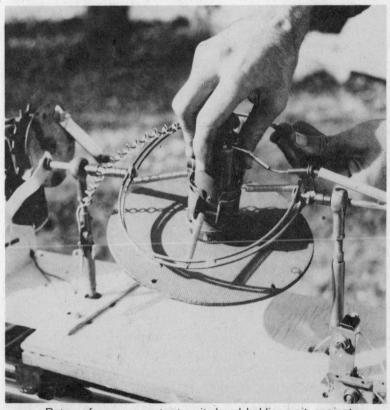

Rotor of gyroscope test unit, hand holding unit against spring tension.

They found that while the rotor did change in weight, it quickly returned to its original weight after it came to rest. They found that when the rotor turned in one direction a force was directed downward, while the opposite rotation produced an upward force.

We believe that had their instrument been constructed similar to ours they would have obtained a trace on the strip chart as we did, and that had their instrument been confined within a pyramid a more drastic result would have been produced on the strip chart.

The fast discharge of weight gain in the Russian experiment may be attributed to the fact that the wheel rotated for only a moment, and the gain or loss of weight was a fleeting one. On the other hand, the tachyon accumulation may be a slow process, as when the ten-pound mass of iron was left inside the pyramid for a period of days and the change in mass was more prolonged. There was a loss of nearly two ounces in the weight, a higher percentage of loss than resulted from the Russian experiment. We attribute this to the fact that inside the pyramid there exists a high concentration of tachyons which are attracted to the atoms of the metal on a gradual basis. This may be speeded up dramatically when the metal is in motion, giving the effect of a large concentration of atoms in any one spot at any given moment. The iron lost weight because of the negative energy present, while in our gyroscope experiment the motion appeared to increase the weight. We did not run tests with the rotor turning in an opposite direction.

The Russian experiments were conducted in a normal laboratory with attendant bright lights, electrical equipment, and more than likely in a conventional square or oblong building, resulting in a minimum or normal flow of tachyons. The pyramid, on the other hand, according to our model, provides a high concentration of tachyons.

The inconsistencies in the Cavendish balance experiments and the gyroscope experiments are not easy at this point in time to resolve.

According to the strip chart readings in the gyroscope experiment, there was either an increase in mass or an increase in speed to give the wave form on the chart. It is also possible that there was an increase in the speed of the rotor and also an increase in weight.

This reasoning does not seem logical from a physical standpoint. If the voltage to the motor is continuous, an increase in the mass of the wheel would result in a slowing of the rotation. On the other hand, a decrease in mass of the rotor would result in an increase in the rotation of the rotor... providing in both cases that the shaft speed would change as the applied load varied. However, in the above cases, the pattern would presumably remain virtually unchanged—the wave form would remain the same since an increase in speed would offset the loss of mass of the rotor.

But we must remember we are dealing with an unknown. Is there such a thing as negative energy and are there tachyons which possess this energy? Is there actually an increase in mass as we know it or does the wheel remain of the same weight and mass but still possess an accumulation of tachyon energy? Would this account for the altered trace on the moving tape, even though the rotor is still moving at the same speed as on the preceding tape?

The Russian experiment indicated that a rotating mass would fall at a different rate according to the direction of rotation. But according to our physics, regardless of the weight, the object would fall at the same rate as another unit of a different mass or weight. So are the Russians encountering some of the problems brought about by the strange tachyon force? Eventually equations may be established which can predetermine the reactions of a moving particle as it passes one point in time and then another point, in turn collecting the negative force of the tachyon in the process.

Taking a look at another area of pyramid research, a forthcoming space probe may provide some new insights on plant behavior within pyramid enclosures.

In *The Secret Power of Pyramids* we described in some detail our experiments with sunflower plants placed inside pyramids and observed over an extended period of time with time-lapse photography. We found that the sunflowers gyrate from west to east in a pronounced arch and completed a cycle every hour and fifty minutes. The plants behaved in this manner only when inside pyramids, while sunflowers placed outside pyramids or in control boxes of shapes other than pyramids moved only slightly. We speculated on the causes of this behavior, and attributed the pronounced movement to increases in energy fields. At that time we believed the energy was of an electromagnetic nature. We still contend that part of the energy can be assigned to the electromagnetic spectrum but we now believe that the unusual forces at play within pyramids are in part due to the presence of tachyons or negative energy.

Plant pathologist Allan H. Brown at the University of Pennsylvania, however, believes the wiggle of the sunflower is due to gravity. He plans to prove or disprove this theory by placing twenty sunflower seedlings on the 1980 U.S.-European Spacelab mission. There the plants will be deprived of gravity and their behavior will be monitored by means of time-lapse photography.

In the meantime, according to a January 3, 1978, Associated Press news article, Brown and associates have been trying the opposite experiment, artificially increasing gravity on growing plants. At sixteen times the force of gravity the plants made the same spiraling motion.

To speculate on the above experiment, it would appear that since the greatly increased gravitational pull on the plants did not alter their dance, something other than gravity is involved. Though an increased gravitational field did not stop the plants from gyrating, we could not detect even the slightest wiggle when an aluminum screen was placed on the west side of the plants inside the pyramid. At least until the Spacelab mission results are forthcoming, we will stick with our own theories concerning energy fields.

Pyramid research has come a long way since the first razor blades were sharpened. The models have grown from six-inch cardboard units to large homes. The latter ensure that the interest in pyramid phenomena will be around for a number of years to come. If we are not closer to the answers, we have at least learned a great deal about how to use the forces involved ... and one can say little more than this about the other forces of nature.

TEN

A Video View of
Pyramid Power

Through visits, letters, phone calls, and during lectures we learned that many people want to do more than speculate on the nature of pyramid energy. While they may enjoy our theories and derive some pleasure from constructing some of their own, what they seem to enjoy most is testing these ideas themselves.

Wanting to become involved in this adventure, they asked us how to build, align, and use pyramids. So, in our books, personal communiques, and scratching on blackboards we have done our best to explain the various steps to them. Trying to make this information as graphic as possible, we were excited when offered the opportunity to make a video film. As often said, a picture is worth a thousand words and we feel this film truly fulfills this assignment.

The viewer does not have to rely on written instuctions or diagrams but can watch, step by step, how to build and set up his own pyramid. A number of experiments are demonstrated and this approach provided us another reason to be excited. A number of these experiments have never been seen on film before. How satisfying it was for us to not only talk about restoring the sharpness razor blades, for example, but to be able to actually show this phenomenon on film, or to allow viewers to see the dancing plants inside pyramids.

Exciting stuff? We think so and believe you will agree with us even more as you become involved in this adventure. In a very real way this exploration is like looking for hidden treasures. These treasures have been buried for thousands of years and the wonder of it all is that as we uncover some jewel from the past it fires our imagination as to the great secrets yet to be discovered. And this treasure hunt does not require the expensive equipment to penetrate formidable deserts and dangerous ocean floors. You can launch your expedition in your home or garage with a few hand tools.

To provide you with a hint of some of the provocative material provided in the film, we have taken some still shots from the show and included them here. As you glance at these imagine, if you will, the experience of seeing these scenes come alive.

The Garvey Center
Research Pyramid

Another View of the
Research Pyramid

These pictures are of the research pyramid (3 stories high) located at the Olive W. Garvey Center for the Improvement of Human Functioning in Wichita, Kansas. This pyramid was built as a replica of the Great Pyramid Cheops (Egypt) as to its dimensions and alignment. A number of experiments in the video program were done at the Center.

A view of the Garvey Center with its
Domed Compound and the Research Pyramid

Medical Testing

Research Library

The Garvey Center is a medical research facility with an out patient clinic capability and an excellent research staff.

Dr. Bill Schul and Co-host Martha Lambert
from the video, "Pyramid Power — A new Reality"

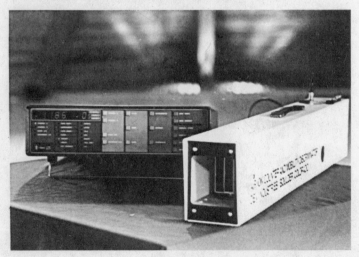

Ion Tester

Dr. Bill Schul and Co-host Martha Lambert conduct an experiment inside the Garvey Pyramid. The bottom photo is the ion generator used to test the air inside the pyramid.

View of a suspended quartz crystal

View of suspended quartz crystal

A large quartz crystal hangs suspended inside the three-story pyramid at the Garvey Center.

The top view is taken from below looking up into the apex of the pyramid. The bottom view is a side angle. The crystal is suspended at the King's Chamber height.

Paul Horn meditating in front
of the Garvey Pyramid

Paul Horn and Martha Lambert
inside the Garvey Pyramid

Jazz and new age musician, Paul Horn, has created a
"new" musical theme for the video program. The theme
was recorded inside the pyramid at the Garvey Center.

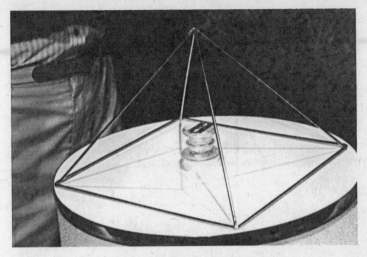

Razor Blade Experiment

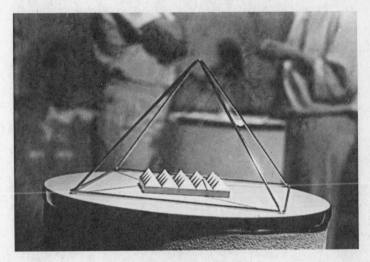

Energy Experiment

Here are two of the many experiments from the video program (1) Re-sharpening of a razor blade (results are microscopically reviewed with amazing results). (2) A pyramid energy plate being tested inside another pyramid.

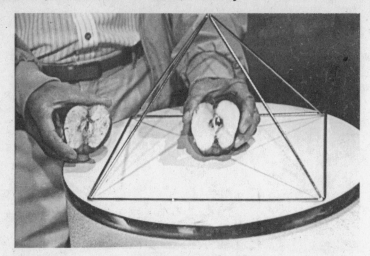

Apple Experiment

Milk Experiment

The testing of food preservation was accomplished by using an apple. One half was kept inside the pyramid and one half outside. The half inside stays fresher on a very consistent basis. The milk tests also validate the longer lasting quality and freshness aspects to pyramid treated foods.

Bill Schul and Martha Lambert with
an experiment.

Bill and Martha with an experiment

Bill Schul and Martha Lambert review some of the
experiments that were visually demonstrated in the video program.

A Martha Lambert Pyramid Meditation

The Mysterious Princess

Martha Lambert (top) inside the Garvey Pyramid is just beginning her meditation.

The mysterious Princess (bottom) seemed to appear out of nowhere. Especially when Martha went into meditation.

BIBLIOGRAPHY

Asimov, Isaac. *Asimov's Guide to Science.* New York: Basic Books, Inc., 1972.
———. *Only a Trillion.* New York: Ace Books, 1976.
Aurobindo, Sri. *The Synthesis of Yoga.* Pondicherry, India: Sri Aurobindo Ashram Trust, 1973.
Bloomfield, H., Cain, M., Jaffe, D., and Rubottom, A. "What Is Meditation?", in *What Is Meditation?*, John White, ed. New York: Doubleday-Anchor, 1974.
Burr, H. S. *Blueprint for Immortality.* London: Neville-Spearman, 1972.
Capra, Fritjof. *The Tao of Physics.* Boulder, Colorado: Shambhala, 1975.
Carlton, James B. "Insights into the Role of Body Energies Through Auric Phenomena." Paper presented at the Ninth Annual Medical Symposium of the A.R.E. Clinic, Inc., Phoenix, Arizona, 1976.
Frei, E. H. "Medical Applications of Magnetism—A New Look at an Archaic Tool," *Bulletin of the Atomic Scientists,* Oct. 1972.
Goodavage, Joseph. *Magic: Science of the Future.* New York: New American Library, 1976.
Griffith, Fred. "Meditation Research: Its Personal and Social Implications," in *Frontiers of Consciousness,* John White, ed. New York: Avon Books, 1975.
Heisenberg, W. *Physics and Philosophy.* New York: Harper Torchbooks, 1958.
Kervran, Louis. *Biological Transmutations.* Brooklyn: Swan House Publishing Co., 1972.
Kilner, Walter. *The Human Aura.* New York: University Books, 1965.
Labes, M. M., quoted by E. H. Frei in "Medical Applications of

Magnetism—A New Look at an Archaic Tool," *Bulletin of the Atomic Scientists*, Oct. 1972.

Linden, W. "The Relation Between the Practicing of Meditation by School Children and Their Levels of Field Dependence-Independence, Test Anxiety and Reading Achievement." Ph.D. dissertation, New York University, 1972.

Murti, T. R. V. *The Central Philosophy of Buddhism*. Hertfordshire, England: George Allen and Unwin, Ltd., 1955.

Nelson, J., Hurwitz, L., and Knapp, D. C. *The Earth's Magnetism*. United States Department of Commerce.

Ostrander, S., and Schroeder, L. *Handbook of Psychic Discoveries*. New York: Berkley Medallion Books, 1975.

———. *Psychic Discoveries Behind the Iron Curtain*. Englewood Cliffs, N.J.: Prentice-Hall, 1970.

Powell, A. E. *The Etheric Double*. Wheaton, Illinois: Theosophical Publishing House, 1925.

Richman, Elliot. "Magnetic 'Halo' Leaks Brain's Top Secret." *Medical Tribune*, Dec. 14, 1977.

Schul, Bill, and Pettit, Ed. *The Psychic Power of Pyramids*. New York: Fawcett Publications, Inc., 1976.

———. *The Secret Power of Pyramids*. New York: Fawcett Publications, Inc., 1975.

Taylor, John. *Superminds*. New York: The Viking Press, Inc., 1975.

Tiller, W. A. "Future Medical Therapeutics Based upon Controlled Energy Fields." Paper presented at the Ninth Annual Medical Symposium of the A.R.E. Clinic, Inc., Phoenix, Arizona, 1976.

Toben, Bob. *Space, Time and Beyond*. New York: E. P. Dutton, 1975.

Tompkins, Peter. *Secrets of the Great Pyramid*. New York: Harper & Row, 1971.

Tompkins, Peter, and Bird, Christopher. *The Secret Life of Plants*. New York: Avon Books, 1973.

United States Coast and Geodetic Survey. *The Magnetism of the Earth*. Publ. 40-1, 1962.

Vivekananda. *Raja Yoga*. New York: Ramakrishna-Vivekananda Center, 1955.

Walker, E. H. "Consciousness and Quantum Theory," in *Psychic Exploration*, Edgar Mitchell, ed. New York: G. P. Putnam's Sons, 1974.

White, John. *Frontiers of Consciousness*. New York: Avon Books, 1975.

INDEX

vibration of, 114, 179
see also plants
centrifugal force, 233
centripetal force, 233
Chauvin, Remy, 126
Chi, 19, 76
China, ancient, 76, 83
Clay, Roger, 29-30
Compton, Arthur H., 54
consciousness, 131-32, 142, 146
cosmic rays, 29-30, 52-53
cosmology, 35-36, 40
  Eastern, 120-21
Cotton, Daisy C., 90-91
Courtney, Albert, 88
Crossley, David, 104
Crouch, Philip, 29-30

Damadian, Raymond, 100
declination, 224-25
dehydration, *see* food
delta brain waves, 159
deltron potential, 83
dematerialization, 178
Design Group Architects, 200
DNA, 57
dowsing, 179
Dyer, Jack, 197

Earth, magnetic field of, 224-25
E.D. Buxton & Associates, 201
Edwards, Jim, 99, 174
Eeman, L.W., 105
Egypt, ancient, 74-76
  see also Great Pyramid of Giza
Einstein, Albert, 74, 131
  on brain, 144
  on imagination, 72
  on photons, 53
  on speed of light, 18, 28, 29
electricity, 50, 53, 81
  animal, 95
  in medicine, 99-104
electrodynamic theory of life, 36, 96
electromagnetic fields
  in life forms, 135-37
  plants and, 244
  in pyramids, 26, 27
  sunspots and, 223

telepathy and, 127, 128
see also magnetic fields
electrons, 53, 54, 240
electrophotography, *see* Kirlian
  photography
energy
  brain's use of, 165
  Einstein on, 28
  life and, 105-11, 115-16
  negative, 243, 244
  positive and negative, 48
  in pyramid-shaped houses, 209, 214-15, 217, 218
  tachyons and, 51-52, 55, 59-60, 69, 83
  universal, 76
  see also electricity
energy fields, 19
  hearing and seeing, 195
  of life, 95
  pyramids for measurement of, 223
  thought as, 36
ESP, *see* telepathy
Esser, Aristide, 173-74
Estebany, Oskar, 97, 98
etheric substance, 81, 82, 133-35
experiments with pyramids, 14-17, 20, 22, 222
  of attraction between masses, 230-33
  using gyroscopes, 233-40
  indented sides and, 21
  using lasers, 45-49, 67-68
  physiological, 93
  using plants, 55-63, 66, 244-45
  of psychic powers, 118, 123-26, 128
  summary of, 31-34
  unexpected results of, 26-27
  using water, 89, 110, 112-13
  weight loss in, 227-30

Falcon, Lou, 170
Feinberg, Gerald, 29
Ficklin, Vicki, 123
food, in pyramid-shaped houses, 194, 207, 212, 213, 216, 218
force fields, 179-80
  see also electromagnetic fields;
    magnetic fields
Franklin, Benjamin, 41